ENDORSEMENTS

I love how Sally Hanan's new book, Empower Yourself, *takes such a unique approach to growing in one's spiritual relationship to God. It is as if you are growing with a wide variety of people through a great number of perspectives because of the quotes from everyday people who have experienced these connections to the Holy Spirit—all very differently from one another. Whether it's prophecy, tongues, or just relating to God's spiritual nature, this tool will bring you all the way into a mature contact with our wonderful Holy Spirit and his gifts. I highly recommend this for all ages and groups to study from.*

~ Shawn Bolz, Senior Pastor
Expression58, Los Angeles
Author of *Translating God* and *Keys to Heaven's Economy*

Sally Hanan has an incarnational gift. She can take the mysteries of the spiritual and make them flesh and blood. Mystics are usually linguistically impaired in communicating deep thoughts, but these are thoughts you can wear on your hands and feet. You can walk this out and be empowered to live so supernaturally that those around you have an encounter with God just because you exist. This book will teach you how. The practice of the principles here will train you if you will apply them. This is the missing manual for living life that you should have been given when you were born, or at least when you were born again.

~ Bill Vanderbush, Associate Pastor
Cathedral of Praise, Austin, Texas
Director, Texas School of Supernatural Ministry, Austin

We want to fully recommend to you Sally Hanan's new book, Empower Yourself. *It's an excellent tool in hearing God speak and in making the gifts of the Holy Spirit and speaking in tongues practical. Sally makes moving in the Spirit and hearing him speak seem so easy and attainable, and you will certainly be equipped, empowered, and activated.*

Be sure to do the interactive journaling at the end of each section. We know you will be hearing and seeing God speak and move in ways you never thought of before, and you will most definitely be launched into a fresh and increased anointing for the works of the kingdom.

~ Jerame and Miranda Nelson, Cofounders
Living At His Feet Ministries
Author (Jerame) of *Encountering Angels, Burning Ones,* and *Manifesting God's Love through Signs, Wonders, & Miracles*
Author (Miranda) of *Take Your Place in the Kingdom*

I have been so blessed by this book. It made me laugh, cry, and drink in revelation all at the same time. I couldn't put it down, and I want everyone in the school and on our prophetic teams to have a copy. Sally Hanan has a beautiful gift of empowering others. She flows in instruction, healing, edification, and prophetic insight. This book is a practical how-to guide that will enable you to bring heaven to earth wherever you go. You will be enlightened and enriched as you read this book and apply the principles to your everyday, ordinary, supernatural life.

~ Sally Curtis, Associate Pastor
Victory Christian Center Houston, Texas
Texas Overseer, Victory School of Supernatural Ministry, Houston

Empower Yourself
IN THE HOLY SPIRIT

Sally Hanan

EMPOWER YOURSELF IN THE HOLY SPIRIT

Copyright © 2015 by Sally Hanan

All rights reserved. No part of this publication may be reproduced, distributed, or transmitted in any form or by any means, including photocopying, recording, or other electronic or mechanical methods, without the prior written permission of the publisher, except in the case of brief quotations embodied in critical reviews and certain other noncommercial uses permitted by copyright law. For permission requests, write to the author, addressed "Attention: Permissions," at the e-mail address below.

Sally Hanan

more@morethanbreathing.com

Special discounts are available on quantity purchases by corporations, associations, and others. Orders by US trade bookstores and wholesalers. For details, contact the author at the e-mail address above.

Unless otherwise marked, all Scripture quotations are from *The Holy Bible, English Standard Version*® (ESV®), copyright © 2001 by Crossway, a publishing ministry of Good News Publishers. Used by permission. All rights reserved.

Quotation from *Translating God: Hearing God's Voice For Yourself and the World Around You* by Shawn Bolz, © 2015 by iCreate Productions. Used by permission. All rights reserved.

Quotation from *The Roar: God's Sound in a Raging World* by Bob Hazlett, © 2013 by Future Coaching Publications. Used by permission. All rights reserved.

Editing services: Inksnatcher & Superior Editing Services
Cover & interior design/layout: Allison Metcalfe Design

First Edition, 2015
ISBN: 978-0-9913350-1-5
Publisher: Fire Drinkers Publishing

This book is dedicated to every single person I have had the pleasure of meeting on this adventure called life. You have each left your mark of love, laughter, or learning on this heart. Thank you for being you.

TABLE OF CONTENTS

FOREWORD IX

I. RELATIONSHIP

1. ANOINTED WITH POWER 1
2. RECOGNIZE HIS VOICE 13
3. SEE AND KNOW 27

II. REVELATION

4. VISIONS AND DREAMS 39
5. PROPHECY 51
6. JUDGING PROPHECY 65

III. REVOLUTION

7. PROPHETIC ARTS 81
8. PHYSICAL HEALING 93
9. INTERCESSION 107

IV. REALITY

10. ALL THE WORLD 121

ABOUT THE AUTHOR

FOREWORD

In my first book, *Fix Yourself,* I take the reader through steps that make the heart whole. When we walk around as wounded soldiers, it's as if we have PTSD—we're always ready for the next hurtful word, the next arrow to pierce our hearts, the next explosion—and with that perspective, it's no surprise when it happens. But when we're whole, we've completely shifted our eyes to focus on the positive, the happy, the good in people. We love fiercely without fear, and we're ready to spy the next piece of gold in others and bring it to the fore. That's what this book is for.

I've split the book into four sections: relationship, revelation, revolution, and reality. I start with an introduction to the Holy Spirit specifically for those who may not be familiar with his ways. Feel free to skip that section, but I wanted to make sure that those reading this as a standalone book wouldn't be thrown in at the deep end if they didn't know him yet. I then give you some tips about how to hear God's voice so as to set the foundation of relationship. The section on revelation teaches you how to understand the messages God sends and then to share his words in a healthy way. Lastly, in the revolution section, I talk about the many ways you can share the gifts of the Holy Spirit with those around you.

Ultimately, God wants people to know him. Sometimes we thirst for the powerful side of the Holy Spirit out of a need to be seen and heard. Most people will see right through that, and God won't necessarily reach hearts that way. The truth is you don't need more gifts, more of a voice, more of anything to be okay as you. You certainly don't need to read this book to be a sign and wonder of the Holy Spirit because you already are, but I hope that in reading it, you will feel more informed and free to minister.

~ Sally

Relationship

ANOINTED WITH POWER

I had been seeking baptism in the Holy Spirit for some time, but the experience kept eluding me. Later I recognized that the Holy Spirit always wanted me to be an active partner, and I would always have to choose to let him move.

I was praying alone in my room, when I saw myself walking through what looked like an old dusty attic (that I knew was my heart). In a dark corner I found a treasure chest that had light glowing out from it, but it was locked with an antique padlock. I found a sword and started trying to pry it open, to no avail. I found myself more and more determined and started hacking at the lock, until it suddenly swung open and light poured into the room. With the light came the first few syllables of my prayer language—not as a gush, more of a trickle. I felt assured, though, that it would develop as I practiced it, just like any language. And it has, as has my relationship with my treasured one.

~ Corey

I was the new Christian reading on the gifts of the Holy Spirit. I told God that if these things were real and true, then I wanted all he had for me. One Sunday during the worship set, he welled up in my chest and throat and I started speaking in tongues and understanding, and then I started praising God.

~ Jalene

A well-known speaker's mom used to have a Bible study I went to. I didn't know what the baptism in the Holy Spirit was at that time, but she put her hand on my forehead. As soon as she put her other hand on me, it felt like being hit with a big gust of wind, and I started speaking in tongues. I didn't know what was happening until they explained it to me later. That day my life was forever changed. I wasn't baptized with water until several years later, but I count that day as the day the Lord claimed me and I claimed him.

~ Birdie

Why do we even need power gifts to reach others? Why can't we use the same things we've been using for centuries—things like Sunday school and theological books, compassion ministries and loving in practical ways?

Well ... because those weren't Jesus's main ministry tools. Most of the details about his short period of ministry are about the miracles he did, not his PowerPoint presentations on how to be a good person. Paul said, "God anointed Jesus of Nazareth with the Holy Spirit and with power. He went about doing good and healing all who were oppressed by the devil" (Acts 10:38). Wouldn't it follow that if God is with us, which he surely is, then we should also be going about doing good and healing *all* who are oppressed?

Paul was on track with Jesus's ministry model: "For I will not venture to speak of anything except what Christ has accomplished through me to bring the Gentiles to obedience—by word and deed, by the power of signs and wonders, by the power of the Spirit of God—so that from Jerusalem and all the way around to Illyricum I have fulfilled the ministry of the gospel of Christ" (Romans 15:18-19). He believed that if he was to minister "in full," if he wanted to fulfill the calling on his life, he had to let the Holy Spirit move through him with signs and wonders, as well as with love and good preaching. In order to experience "the fullness of him who fills all in all" (Ephesians 1:23), Paul prayed that we'd clearly see and flow in the immeasurable greatness of his power (with the same supreme authority that raised Christ from the dead). Therefore, the fullness of our walk with Christ has to include a willingness to move in signs and wonders too.

Jesus made a big deal out of giving the twelve disciples "power and authority over all demons and to cure diseases," and he said that the proclaiming of the kingdom of God should be accompanied by healing (see Luke 9:1-2). A life of ministry is about the life in our feet, hands, hearts, and minds. Are we flowing from heaven to earth, or are we telling God how it will be based on our comfort levels? It's not that we all have to run out in the streets speaking in tongues, but we *do* have to live in him, and that means flowing from his heart and Spirit to offer the life and love he carries.

The results can be dramatic, as seen in the lives of Rolland and Heidi Baker, the founders of Iris Global, who moved to Mozambique in 1995 to bring the love of God to the poorest of the poor. They credit the explosive growth of their ministry to the leading of the Holy Spirit. Today they feed over 10,000 children a day, and Iris's church network numbers more than 10,000. Of the members of those church families, 90 percent said they became interested in knowing Jesus when they saw the miracles done in his name.

We have seen repeatedly over the years that Christian growth and power for service are functions of the sheer power of the Holy Spirit, and that power can be imparted with astounding speed. More can be accomplished overnight in the Spirit than many experience in entire, lengthy discipleship programs. One vision can change an entire life. One glimpse of Jesus' face can change everything. One look into hell can change every priority. One taste of heaven and all attraction for the things of this world is lost. We should not and cannot underestimate what God can do to transform the most unlikely and undeserving people in a flash. In Iris we have seen callous, numb, uncaring souls changed into new creations overnight. We are especially seeing a new generation of young believers receiving impartations and visitations we older leaders never dreamed of at that age. Our values lead us to ask and expect all the more from God in the way of priceless impartations of every good gift from His hands, but always seeking His face more than His hands.[1]

~ Rolland Baker, Cofounder and Director, Iris Global

We have the tools of effective ministry lying on the table in front of us. It's up to us to pick them up and use them. The power in the words of Scripture is the same power needed to reach the heart, mind, and body today. There's life in everything God does, so why would he kill off one of his greatest signs of life—his power to restore mental and physical health and to encourage the soul? Exactly—he wants us to move in his power with all engines on … but that requires a relationship with him.

When we know a person, we are pretty good at figuring out what that person is thinking or likely to do next. When married, we get to such a deep and intimate level of knowing that we start to finish each other's sentences, or we get up to make that cup of tea before it's asked for.

It's the same way with God. The more time we spend in his presence, the more we get to know his heart and what's on his mind. The Holy Spirit delights in sharing God's secrets and mysteries (see Ephesians 3:3-5 and Daniel 4:9), and just like any retreat or vacation, the more time we spend with the Holy Spirit, the more we get to know him intimately.

None of it can flow freely unless we have the key that unlocks that door of intimacy. Which begs the question: Have you been filled with the Holy Spirit?

---

1. https://www.irisglobal.org/news/newsletters/view/our-ministry-outlook-at-iris

There's no mystery formula to this; you simply open the door. and ask him to come in. Sometimes fear is attached to the thought of being filled with the presence of God, so don't feel bad if you're experiencing fear while reading this. I was scared too—scared that God would take away what little of a good life I thought I had—but I was determined. I'd seen his presence light up others and I wanted it too. I knew my life would be full of perfect light and love once I was open to it. And then I *was* open to it and it was perfect.

When you minster to others, you're either plugged into the Holy Spirit or you're not. Flowing with the Holy Spirit is not about some pixie dust feeling, although many have reported feeling something. It's about having the Spirit of God in union with your spirit and operating from that place of unity.

> *It's also about being in unity with others. Shortly after the Pentecost experience in the upper room, the believers assembled again (obviously one taste wasn't enough) and asked God to continue to help them speak his words boldly and accompany them with healing, signs, and wonders. God's response was to fill everyone present with the Holy Spirit (see Acts 4:29). What followed in the weeks after was an incredible display of how a community of believers can operate in agape, or self-sacrificial love. Having the Holy Spirit not only serves your spirit; he also flows outward to everyone around you to do what he does best through you—serve in love.*

TONGUES

If you think of the Trinity as a perfect family, the Holy Spirit has a hefty role—he helps, teaches, comforts, advocates, intercedes, and empowers us. Our efforts to do any of those things without him will be devoid of the fullness he gives. Inviting him in just makes sense.

Many times, that invitation includes the gift of tongues. Some would say that if you can't speak in tongues, you don't have the Holy Spirit. That's a stretch, even though many people do receive it at the same time as being filled with the Holy Spirit. Tongues are a separate *gift*. It showed up at Pentecost *because it was needed that day* to minister to the crowds (see Acts 2:4), and it showed up in Ephesus, along with the gift of prophecy, because *it was needed that day* to minister to the Jews and Greeks (see Acts 19:6 and 10). That's the beauty of having the Holy Spirit in you—he shows up in whatever form necessary to minister to those who need him *in the moment*.

In her memoir *Chasing the Dragon,* Jackie Pullinger wrote about her initial years of struggle ministering in the slums of Hong Kong's Walled City without the power she needed. One night she asked God to give her whatever he had that would help her to make Jesus real to the lost, because her words and actions weren't enough. She was immediately filled with the Holy Spirit's power and began speaking in tongues, and her ministry changed overnight from one of powerlessness to one of countless miracles and salvations. She stated that we have to let Jesus be the one to reveal himself through us at a Spirit-to-spirit level or we miss the whole point of Christianity.

Tongues are a wonderful gift. Some say that tongues are for expressing deep emotions we have no words for, while others say they're for intercessory purposes—we can slam the devil with fighting words straight from heaven. I have a theory though: If you stand by someone speaking in tongues and you recognize the language, you'll invariably hear words of worship and praise overflowing from within (see Acts 2:11 and Acts 10:46).

What if every deep emotion and prayer spoken in tongues is sent up in the form of worship? What if that's the secret weapon to destroying the devil's plans? Sometimes I'm in the middle of a bad day and I start speaking in tongues to get out of my funk. Wouldn't it make perfect sense that worshiping in tongues is the key to realigning your spirit with heaven? Ever since I've thought this, praying in tongues just makes me happy.

I've heard numerous testimonies of people being healed or saved simply by someone praying in tongues over them. There's power in the outpouring of the Holy Spirit from your mouth. You're releasing unknown words from heaven into the atmosphere on earth and changing its dynamics. Sometimes you'll feel peace, sometimes an urge to yell, sometimes joy, but because your spirit is in tune with the Holy Spirit, you're releasing the goodness of God.

Speaking in tongues is a useful tool when you don't know what to pray, or you're feeling disconnected from God and you want a tune-up. All you have to do is open your mouth and let your spirit merge with the Holy Spirit to set you right. So if the first thing that happens when the Holy Spirit ignites within you is the eruption of heavenly praise in an unknown language, then you are doubly blessed.

Don't be afraid. When fear holds you back, you're comparable to a bank account a friend has deposited millions of dollars into, and you're unwilling to make a withdrawal because you're afraid of your ways of spending. What a waste! So when I talk about flowing in the gifts of the Holy Spirit, it's not just for you, it's for mankind. Are you ready to save the world? Read on!

TRUTH

What is the truth about the Holy Spirit in us? Mull over the following Scriptures and write down anything God shows you through them.

"God anointed Jesus of Nazareth with the Holy Spirit and with power. He went about doing good and healing all who were oppressed by the devil, for God was with him" (Acts 10:38).

"The Holy Spirit fell on all who heard the word. And the believers from among the circumcised who had come with Peter were amazed, because the gift of the Holy Spirit was poured out even on the Gentiles. For they were hearing them speaking in tongues and extolling God" (Acts 10:44).

"I baptize you with water for repentance, but he who is coming after me is mightier than I, whose sandals I am not worthy to carry. He will baptize you with the Holy Spirit and fire" (Matthew 3:11).

"And suddenly there came from heaven a sound like a mighty rushing wind, and it filled the entire house where they were sitting. And divided tongues as of fire appeared to them and rested on each one of them. And they were all filled with the Holy Spirit and began to speak in other tongues as the Spirit gave them utterance" (Acts 2:1-4).

"Being therefore exalted at the right hand of God, and having received from the Father the promise of the Holy Spirit, he has poured out this that you yourselves are seeing and hearing" (Philippians 2:3-4).

FINISH THESE SENTENCES

I think the Holy Spirit looks like

I think the Holy Spirit feels like

I want/don't want the Holy Spirit to have full access to me because

I want/don't want the Holy Spirit to minister in any way he wants through me because

When I think about having the Spirit of God in union with my spirit and operating from that place of unity, I

I think the gift of tongues is

BE FILLED

If you read the book of Acts, you'll notice that some were filled with the Holy Spirit the second they said yes to Jesus. Others did everything in stages, and it seems to be the same today. I have no idea why, but I suspect it may be to do with our level of skepticism, which is why it took *me* so long to say yes ... .

The Holy Spirit knows when you're ready for him because you're willing to ask. Place yourself in a setting that feels comfortable and tell him you'd like him to come and fill you up. Then wait a moment.

Or join other Christians and ask them to lay hands on you for the baptism in the Holy Spirit.

Know that you won't necessarily feel anything or burst into tongues, but you've asked and received in faith, and now you are full of the Holy Spirit.

"I was not sure it was real or that I had even been filled with the Holy Spirit until I started standing in front of people and was filled with "words" for them. It wasn't general stuff like, "I feel like there is pain in your past with your family and God wants you to know that he loves you" stuff, I had very specific encouraging words for people. God would give me his perspective of love on their thoughts and struggles to share with them. It was when I saw their reactions to extremely specific details about their lives and God's words following that I realized the Holy Spirit was real and I was able to hear him."
~ John

"I was depressed and miserable. I had a daydream that I was in this black hole looking for a pinpoint of light to show the way out, but it was all black. My grandpa's Bible was in my room. I got on my knees in front of the window and prayed. I don't know how this unchurched girl knew this word, but I prayed, "Lord, am I an abomination to you?" I opened the Bible and this verse jumped out at me: "All who practice these things are an abomination to me." Well, that tripped me out, because he answered me, and at the same time this incredible love enveloped me, and it was so amazing! It was the Holy Spirit, and I was never the same."
~ Crista

SPEAK IN TONGUES

Some people get very upset over the fact that they can't speak in tongues. There's nothing wrong with you if you don't. You're not inadequate in any way. There's nothing you've done that made God point his big stick at you and say, "That one, give him nothing." He's just not like that.

Nevertheless, here are some helpful things you can do to encourage the gift to flow:

Don't overthink it. Sometimes we're so into our rational thoughts we turn off our spiritual entry points.

Turn up the worship music. It always helps us to relax and get into the flow of the Spirit.

Start to say any sort of anything that comes out of your mouth. Where the Spirit of the Lord is, there is freedom. Give yourself permission to sound ridiculous for a few minutes (much easier when you're alone!).

Try singing out the sounds that fill your mouth. It can be easier than listening to yourself babble.

"I grew up in church and was confirmed, but I kept going back and forth between God and whomever and whatever. Some hippie friends got saved and Spirit-filled and pushed some books (no clue which ones, but by one of the prominent early '70s' charismatic authors) about the Holy Spirit on me. I was longing deep down for what I saw in the Bible, especially the New Testament, so I prayed by the formula laid out in the books. God, in his infinite mercy, honored my innocent following of that advice and filled me. I'd had a relationship off and on with God, and when his presence was manifest, I was overwhelmed by love. I felt that anew.

The signs of his having filled me were definitely there: I could speak in tongues like nobody's business, sometimes got interpretations, and got words for others. I could see in the Spirit some things that were about to happen. I couldn't make that stuff up."

~ Miles

Notes

Anointed with Power

10

Notes

RECOGNIZE HIS VOICE 2

As a child, I felt him in the wind. Thunder also turned my attention to him. At age six, I remember having conversations with God while playing outside.

~ Traci

I lived in Southern California. The beach, mountains, desert, and other trips were the norm for my family. Sitting in the woods and seeing and hearing all the birds and the creek nearby, I could see God's peace. In the desert, I saw his provision and wonder. At the beach, I saw his power. Going fishing in the early morning, I felt his presence, and that was long before I understood what I was sensing.

~ Dawn

God's mostly silent to me, but I guess sometimes I experience what people call "knowing" through reading or recalling the Word, praying, or listening to worship music. Maybe I hear an occasional inner voice, but then, I hear a lot of those. Every once in a while, I suspect one is probably God. I don't know the first time that a certain "knowing" became fact for me, but it was likely when the way to salvation was explained to me as a child. A few more recent experiences that turned my belief into more of a walk (or at least a crawl) were during a casual group study of Proverbs, and hearing "The Change" by Stephen Curtis Chapman for the first time.

~ Cathy

Sometimes I'll be going about my day and suddenly someone will pop into my head. Then the thought might occur to me that I haven't heard from her in a while, so I should call. Invariably, I'll find that she's in a certain life situation in which she needs to know that God is with her and he cares and understands. My out-of-the-blue call confirms that he is and he does, and I'll get to pray with her and be Jesus with skin on.

~ Elizabeth

I grew up in a very abusive home with yelling, screaming, and degradation every day, so for me, it's not just what the Holy Spirit says but how he says it. He always speaks in such a way that it moves me at the very core of who I am.

~ David

Getting to know God is never instant, but when you regularly bathe in the presence of the Holy Spirit, it's as if you've been in a dark house and suddenly it floods with light. Beginning a relationship with God is just like the first few exciting dates with someone. You begin by learning everything you can about him. You probably devour the Bible, find yourself hanging out with other believers as often as possible, and then ... sometimes ... you get discouraged, because all those happy Christians can hear God talking to them and you can't. This may bring up the question: *Is there something wrong with me?*

Absolutely not! God doesn't create seconds. We are all created perfectly different, so it follows that there is no singular path to knowing what God is thinking, saying, and doing. Different aspects of his presence in us stir our souls and speak to us, and it takes a while to practice the awareness of them all over present realities.

Some pastors joke that we are so heavenly minded, we are of no earthly use, but I disagree. To be aware of the voice and presence of God at all times is to be open to all of heaven's possibilities in a moment. Apparently we become the thing we focus on, and we take on the perspectives of those we surround ourselves with. It's a matter of choice, albeit a difficult one. It does take a bit of mental effort to switch thinking patterns from a place of logical thinking to one that's less concrete, but as C.S. Lewis puts it so beautifully:

> *"If I find in myself desires which nothing in this world can satisfy, the only logical explanation is that I was made for another world."* ~ C.S. Lewis, *Mere Christianity*

So if God talks through intangible things, how can we focus on them? Some people learn by watching friends' responses to conflict, happy moments, or tragedy. They read about Jesus's responses to friends and enemies, and they can hear and see testimonies unfolding when they watch the Holy Spirit work through others. Other people have an internal *knowing*. They just *know* that God is near, or he is holding them, or he is laughing with them.

Others are feelers—they can feel God's emotions of pleasure or sadness. When Spirit-filled people pray for them, they can feel peace flow through them. To some, everything stills for a few seconds. For others, it feels like water rushing through their bodies. It's an internal sense rather than an external one. Others are seers—they can *see* pictures of God in action around or in them. It's very like daydreaming, in that the pictures in their heads are of things they may or may not be familiar with.

All of these tools of awareness are developed over time as we become aware of God's particular ways of talking with us, but it takes practice. I have yet to meet someone who has had an instant download of perfectly detailed communication the moment he or she said yes to God. It's taken me about thirty years, so go easy on yourself. Awareness and hearing God is a long-term, heart-to-heart journey.

> *Are you mostly a seer, a feeler, or a knower? God is in you and with you right now. Do you feel his presence, or can you "see" him, or do you simply "know" he's there?*

NATURE

Hearing God has been a natural progression for me, starting with nature. For most of us, being outdoors and watching nature was our first and most concrete sense of the presence and beauty of God. I'd lie on the grass and track the moving clouds; I'd climb trees; I'd listen intently to the mix of wind and birds and swishing leaves, just like this friend:

> *"I grew up in SoCal, a busy place full of people and traffic and noise. Sonic booms rained down from the skies almost daily, thanks to the Naval Air Station. I can remember them from as far back as kindergarten. As a teenager, I began to explore the foothills and the mountains. I found places that rose above the squalor of city life, where nature seemed to place a magic blanket over the noise below. It was there, resting on lonely precipices that jutted out over the wilderness, that I began to realize the God of my little New Testament (won as a prize from the backyard Bible school I attended in the fifth grade) was also the God of this. This, an unruly wilderness full of snakes and bears and cougars. This, a place of solitude and peace. This, a place where the air smelled of pines and the sunset was dusted with pale pinks and yellows. Sitting on those jutting rocks, I began to understand the artistry of God and the intricate ways he displays his majesty. It was there, in the hallowed places where eagles nest, that I began to speak to him, to ask my hard questions, to test his ability to meet me there in my own wilderness. I've traveled far since then, but our conversations experienced in the beauty of his creation have never left me. I've hidden*

them in the more sacred places of my heart, where only I can unlock them."

~ Birdie

And Rebecca:

"I began to experience God at summer camp as an eight-year-old kid. Nightly, during our worship times in the open air, I would breathe in as the wind blew and imagine the Lord breathing into me. I let everything that was not of him leave as I exhaled and sang. I felt him all around."

~ Rebecca

These days, it's not much of a stretch to see, hear, and feel God in the beauty around me. A cloud might show up through my windshield in the shape of a cliff, and I'll get the message that it's time to take a leap of faith. A tree might drop all its leaves in a few days, and I'll know God's telling me to let some things go that I thought mattered and that everything has its day. I might hold a pecan in my hand and marvel over the mottling on its shell, and I'll hear God whisper that his design of me is far more intricate.

One touch of nature unites us with God's heart in a powerful way. Read Tony's story:

"In 1988, having just suffered the loss of my bride to a drunk driver on our honeymoon, I would regularly go out to the little country cemetery which had a nearby manmade lake and a beautiful view. Every time I went out there, a breeze would blow across the lake. It was so comforting. I called it the breath of God. One day I was sitting next to my wife's grave, and some of the flowers had blown out of the vase on her stone. Along with the silk flowers was a little ornamental bird that had also fallen out. I planted the flowers back in the vase and set the little bird back on top. I remember this well: I looked down at the stone and once again sobbed at the loss of my bride. I said, 'God, what is going to happen with my life?' Just then, the wind blew the little bird off the stone again, and God said, 'Not one sparrow falls to the ground unnoticed by me. How much more will I take care of you?'"

~ Tony

JOURNALING

So how did I learn to *get a message* or *know* or *hear*? I've always had a hankering to know it all, which is why I went on my quest to hear God all those years ago, and it started with journaling. I had so many thoughts swirling around my head at unacceptable times of the day and night that it made sense to try and laser them onto paper in order to subject them to a more rational thought process. Every day or so, I'd sit with my Bible and notebook and write my thoughts to God about a Bible verse I'd just read. Then I'd wait for whatever I thought he was saying back and write it down.

I'd go back through what I'd just written and see how much of it came from me and how much of it was from God. I thought it would be really difficult to distinguish God's voice, but it was quite easy in the end. Everything that was kind wasn't mine. (Yes, I hated myself back then.) I always added a little humor and snarkiness to my journal entries, because I wanted to be real with him, and I found he spoke back to me in my language.

"One touch of nature makes the whole world kin." ~ Shakespeare, *Troilus and Cressida,* Act III, Scene iii

The more we respond to God according to our "bent"—the healthy aspects of the filter we do life through—the better we get at communicating. We can respond to him in our peculiar or unique ways and begin to flow freely with him and see heaven flow on earth through us.

SEEING

Being raised in Ireland had distinct advantages, the main one being my constant fare of Irish myths and legends. We all knew and visualized the stories of children being turned into swans, bad fairies, magic harps, and wish-granting leprechauns. We were encouraged to use our imaginations to the max, and we did. All that visualization meant I got to practice at the kingdom level early on, and I've always been a daydreamer, conjuring up pictures in my mind of what could have or should have happened, or of unfolding stories I would write for English homework. Of all the ways I recognize God's voice, seeing is probably the easiest for me.

Everyone can *see* though. I'll prove it to you. Hold out your hand and imagine an empty ice cream cone in it. Now picture the ice cream. Congratulations—you've just *seen* something.

> *Daniel was a seer, and one of the reasons he was so good at it was that he had years of experience. Not only did he accept the first picture he got, he went on to see detail after detail until he was satisfied he had seen everything there was to see.*

You can do this too. Think back to that ice cream. Is the cone textured or smooth? What flavor is the ice cream? Is it one scoop or two? Is the cone lined with chocolate? Are there sprinkles on the ice cream? What color are they? Is there anything else about the ice cream that stands out? Now lift the ice cream up to your mouth and have some.

Not only have you imagined this ice cream, you've also integrated knowledge and experience with your creative imagination to such a degree that you could almost taste the ice cream. You can see almost anything on command—a red poppy, a sheet of papers a castle. You can see these because you already know in your head what they should look like. But like the artist who develops her talent, it takes practice drawing in front of the real thing to capture its full essence. She notices the light and shade, the angles, the lines. She learns how to capture it all and draw the real thing. It's the same way with *seeing* what God is showing you. It takes practice. We are all capable of imagining. And there's nothing wrong with it … unless you are on a diet (re visualizing ice cream. Sorry!).

The more I practice this form of hearing God, the easier it becomes to filter out the *me* and zoom in on the parts of it that God is highlighting. It's somewhat harder to see things you have no grid for, which is why some people's stories of heaven and visions seem so out there, but God is trying to connect with you and show you things that will lead you into more intimacy with him. Sometimes God's weirdness and sense of humor will cause you to see weird and funny things, so be open to everything you see and trust that his heart message to you will be meaningful.

CLUES

I meet a lot of people who say they don't see or hear or feel anything at all, but there are many ways to hear God. As I mentioned before, you can build up your *knowing* by reading and meditating on Bible verses and by hearing the testimonies of God at work through other people. Jesus promised that we would never be alone and that we'd have the Holy Spirit with us at all times, so why is it so difficult? Actually, God is great at giving us clues; he helps us to see more into everyday objects and thoughts with a bit of practice, as Hae Ryung discovered:

"Hearing God's voice is just natural to me, especially now that I've studied natural sciences. I guess I first noticed his voice in the classroom. It's been a very interesting journey, because when observing nature in all its glory, I see God everywhere. Since I've been studying cancer, I'm seeing the sin nature and how the corrupted side really goes against God's design. The spiritual realm and the natural realm are so amazingly and intricately woven together."

—Hae Ryung

"If you want to know what God is saying, have a thought!"
~ Bill Vanderbush

RECOGNIZE HIS VOICE

Tracking clues could be the easiest way to hear God, because the clue is right in front of you or in your hand, so let's do this:

Just as you did in our ice cream cone exercise, you'll study the detail of an object in front of you. For example, I have a coffee mug on my desk. Its main colors are yellow and red. It has a mouse holding a cup and standing on a podium, and there are mice in the background cheering for him. Once I've noticed the details, I tune in to the Holy Spirit to *see, hear, know,* and *sense.*

The very first sense I get is that God is very happy I'm finally writing these things down and sharing them with you. (He's been on my case for quite some time.) I notice that stars are all around the top of the cup, which means that this is not the last time he'll have me write things that help others. This comes to me as a *knowing.* And then I turn the cup around and start to laugh, because written on that side are the words, "It's no good trying to hide it anymore." There's no need to decipher that.

Just as he did with my mug, I find that most of the time God speaks to encourage me and push me—both into my future and closer to his heart. You will probably find the same. It's when we're desperate that we can miss the message, because we are convinced it will come as a louder voice than all the others. If it's a life-changing *don't do that or you'll miss your entire destiny* kind of decision, you'll usually know the answer before even trying to find it. We all have an internal compass that guides us to the Father's heart. Sometimes the answer and direction you need is close by—consult a few wise, godly people you know for advice, so that even if you can't hear a definitive answer from God, you won't go far off from the right decision.

TRUTH

What is the truth about our ability to hear God? Mull over the following Scriptures and write down anything God shows you through them.

"Oh, taste and see that the LORD is good!" (Psalm 34:8).

"There shall come forth a shoot from the stump of Jesse, and a branch from his roots shall bear fruit. And the Spirit of the LORD shall rest upon him, the Spirit of wisdom and understanding, the Spirit of counsel and might, the Spirit of knowledge and the fear of the LORD. And his delight shall be in the fear of the LORD. He shall not judge by what his eyes see, or decide disputes by what his ears hear" (Isaiah 11:1-3).

"He who has an ear, let him hear what the Spirit says to the churches" (Revelation 2:29).

"The proverbs of Solomon, son of David, king of Israel: To know wisdom and instruction, to understand words of insight" (Proverbs 1:1).

"For what can be known about God is plain to them, because God has shown it to them. For his invisible attributes, namely, his eternal power and divine nature, have been clearly perceived, ever since the creation of the world, in the things that have been made" (Romans 1:19-20).

FINISH THESE SENTENCES

I think I mostly hear God through

I want/don't want to let God develop my spiritual senses because

I would love to develop my ability to (choose one) see/think/know/feel God because

When I think about having ongoing conversations with God, I

I think I might have missed God's voice in the past because

For the next few days, I'm going to start paying more attention to

NATURE

Head outdoors and settle into a cozy spot.

See everything—trees, clouds, foliage, grass, hills, birds. Notice the beauty of each minuscule detail and thought put into it all. Notice the colors, shapes, layers, and levels. Think about the kind of artist who could come up with such an amazing design. What is God showing you?

Listen to every tiny noise around you. What is God saying?

RECOGNIZE
HIS
VOICE

Sense the presence and power of creation. Feel the peacefulness. What is he giving you?

Know the presence of an imaginative and loving Creator. What thoughts or Scriptures come to mind?

Smell the unending number of fragrances. What do those fragrances link your thoughts to?

When you look at the birds, when you taste good food, when a line in a movie stands out—dwell on them. When you live in the awareness of the constant presence of God, you can't help but hear and see him all the time.

Some people say that hearing God is about paying attention to your thoughts. When I started doing that, I discovered many of my thoughts were not my own, which makes me suspect that God is talking to us far more often than we think.

THOUGHTS

Practice hearing from your spirit. Write here, over the next day or week, things you notice that stand out.

NAMES

SONG LYRICS

BIBLE VERSES

SOMETHING YOU HEARD SOMEONE SAY TODAY

TASTES

SMELLS

COLORS

SOUNDS

REPETITIVE SIGNS OR VISUALS

Notes

Recognize His Voice

Notes

Recognize His Voice

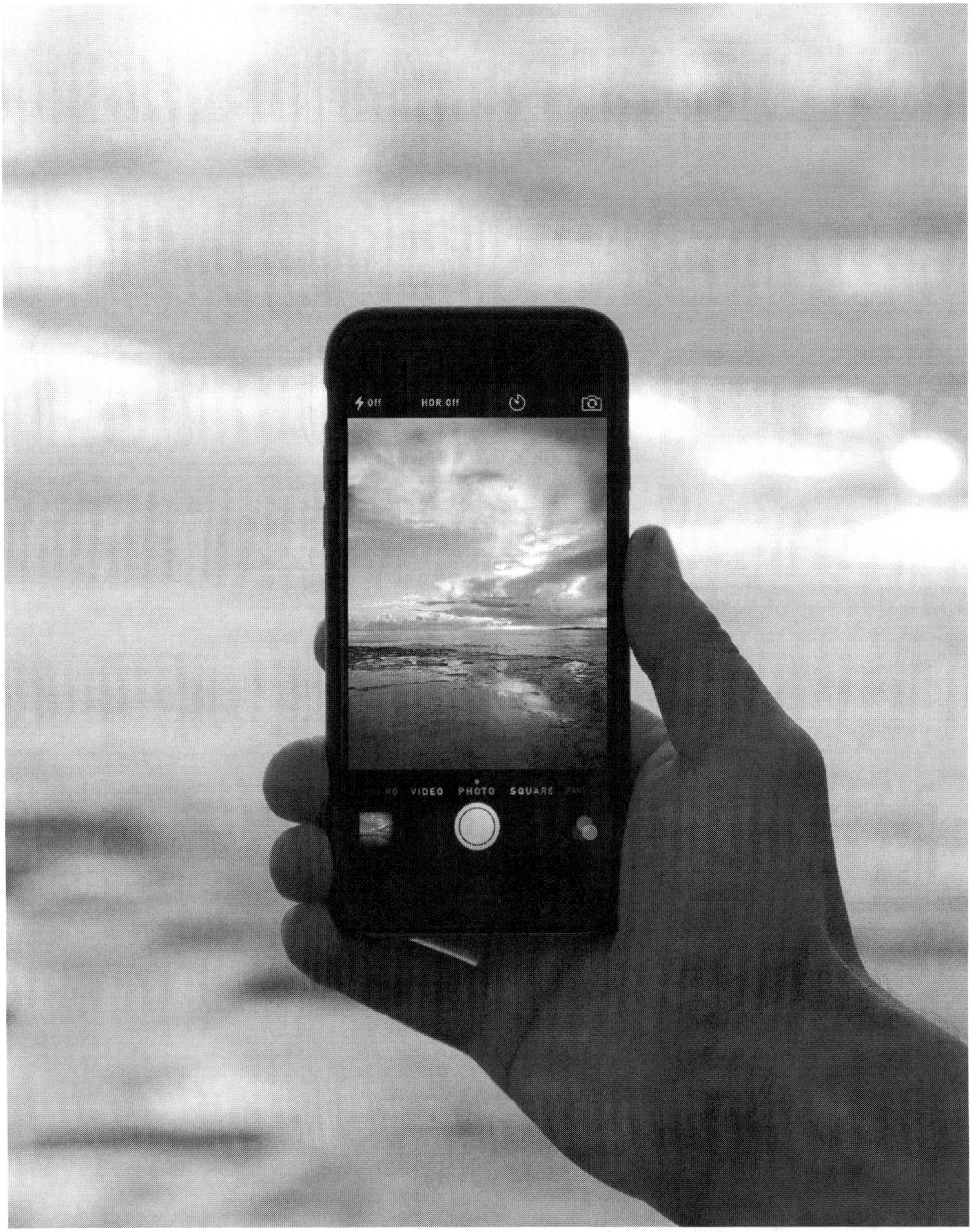
Off
HDR Off
VIDEO
PHOTO
SQUARE

See and Know

I love the Holy Spirit's patience. He just won't give up trying to communicate with us. When we miss it one way, he comes at it from another angle. When he wants to say something, it's amazing to experience the lengths to which he will go. I really love that part of the adventure.

~ Joseph

For years it was, in the words of Larry Niven, thoughts that materialized with "crystalline certainty." I'd realize I knew something, as if I had known it for years, studied it, and experienced it. Solid truth just sitting there. That still happens, but now it's somewhat more likely to be a voice. It's almost never audible, but it might as well be. This may come out of the blue or as part of a conversation. The conversation may be directly with God, or it may start out as an imagined conversation with someone else as a way to examine things, when BAM!

~ Miles

When he speaks, I just know. There's no way to describe it. It's like feeling the sun or the wind; you know it by the quality.

~ Tracey

He speaks to me in many ways, from seeing a butterfly at the age of seventeen to an audible voice at the age of fifty-four. Sometimes it's a knowing or intuitive feeling. Sometimes it's through others—either they say something or I read something they've written.

~ Bobbi

The Holy Spirit constantly surprises me. Just when I think I have a clear understanding of what, where, how, or why, I am thrown for a loop and humbled by how much I have underestimated him.

~ Brenda

I'm not sure when I started to notice, but he sends me special presents. I've seen a white deer, an eagle on a back road, a special plant in my front window. Every day I feel like he's sending me flowers. These are just some of the gifts. To others it might not mean much, but for me, I know he's thinking of me.

~ Tina

As with any relationship, we listen to, hear, and strive to understand those we love. Given that we've evolved historically from a life of working the fields to the tech world we live in today, we are going to have a large number of possible distractions and random thoughts that upset communication.

The heart wants what the heart wants, and our hearts want to be one with God—so closely entwined that we can hear him breathe and think and laugh. After all, that's what he died for (John 14-17). If you're discouraged because you're nowhere close to hearing God, I'd like to encourage you by letting you know that I have never met anyone, in my twenty-plus years of inner healing and coaching, who could not hear, sense, feel, or know God in some way after a little inspiration. Perhaps you're concerned you're being deceived in the things you've heard. Here's a plumb line for you:

Is it good? Is it kind? Is it encouraging?

Does it make you want to get closer to God or farther from him?

DIRECT COMMUNICATION

In the Old Testament, prophets received the word of the Lord. In the New Testament (and today), prophetic people *perceived* the word of the Lord. The OT prophets received a direct download and they were just vessels, but the NT prophets were perceivers. Some Christians have trained themselves to think that their relationship with God has to be like a church service in the '50s—"Sit down, shut up, and never expect a discussion." Give yourself room to practice hearing him and making mistakes. Who would expect a husband to know what his new wife is thinking in the first years of marriage? God doesn't expect that with him either.

Part of God's joy is that you're getting to know his heart for you and those around you, and he loves to send little surprises your way to help you along. Take the lyrics of the song "Give It Away" by the Red Hot Chili Peppers. Perhaps the chorus just dropped into your mind and you have no idea why, and you're bothered because "Give it away, give it away now" is very far from the words you wanted in your head. But then you dutifully look up the lyrics to see what there could possibly be of any value in such a secular song. Well, well, lookee here: You're born into the river of life as a giver, full of the warmth of his eternal love for you, and it's time to pass that love on.

I would assume, based on that last example, that right now you're thinking about something you previously heard, saw, or thought about that you realize may have been God speaking to you. Perhaps he talked to you through your Bible reading this morning, but you're not sure. That's when I write him notes. For example, I can flick to this verse: "Beloved, do not be surprised at the fiery trial when it comes upon you to test you, as though something strange were happening to you. But rejoice insofar as you share Christ's sufferings, that you may also rejoice and be glad when his glory is revealed" (1 Peter 4:12). Then I start writing.

God,

This one always riles me up, because there are so many people who think that when someone's mean to them, it's because it's a "fiery trial from Satan." No! It's more likely that the mean person is a jerk, or that the Christians are so weird, they make everyone around them nervous. They're not suffering for you! They're not suffering because they're Christians! Sigh.

But then you're talking about something testing me. Even though you don't test us, you do let life happen. We don't get to stay all wrapped up in Bubble Wrap like the children of the smother mothers. We get to grow our hearts through experience so we can repeatedly choose a "more excellent way." And I didn't do so well on that one, did I? It took me three years to apologize to "her." Ahem. And then your glory was finally revealed. Ahem again.

Point taken. Game, set, and match to God (as usual).

Sally

Or what if you're at your computer, supposedly right in the middle of a very important assignment, and you keep getting distracted. You look up to see the words "No Spacing" at the top of your page. You know it's God telling you to stop spacing out. You chuckle at his humor and ask him for a real word a few minutes later, and go figure, you look up to see "Subt ... , which in God-speak means *Oh, you want me to be more subtle then? How about no? How about getting back to that assignment already?* Not that I'd know anyone that happened to ....

Or you walked into your backyard this morning and saw a squirrel staring right at you with an acorn in his hands, and he didn't move for a long time. In your heart of hearts, you know it was God's way of telling you that despite your financial difficulties, he's with you.

God really is always talking. It's up to us to perceive him, which involves our minds, our imaginations, and our perceptions. The hearing problem is on our end. All it takes on our part is more awareness, more practice, and the willingness to live from heaven to earth instead of from earth to heaven. Let's enjoy the journey as we learn how to "live and move and have our being" in him (Acts 17:28).

TRUTH

What is the truth about using our senses to hear God? Mull over the following Scriptures and write down anything God shows you through them.

"That they may all be one, just as you, Father, are in me, and I in you, that they also may be in us, so that the world may believe that you have sent me. The glory that you have given me I have given to them, that they may be one even as we are one" (John 17:20-22).

"And you will feel secure, because there is hope; you will look around and take your rest in security" (Job 11:18).

SEE AND KNOW

"They have hands, but do not feel; feet, but do not walk; and they do not make a sound in their throat" (Psalm 115:7).

"And he made from one man every nation of mankind … that they should seek God, and perhaps feel their way toward him and find him. Yet he is actually not far from each one of us, for 'In him we live and move and have our being'" (Acts 17:26-28).

"As servants of God we commend ourselves in every way: … by purity, knowledge, patience, kindness, the Holy Spirit, genuine love; by truthful speech, and the power of God" (2 Corinthians 6:4-8).

FINISH THESE SENTENCES

Are the things I think God is saying
good,
kind,
encouraging?

My understanding of the difference between receiving a word vs. perceiving one is

When hearing God, I think he expects me to

When I think most of my random thoughts could be God talking to me, I

I'm willing/not willing to let God talk to me through my mind, imagination, and/or perceptions because

WRITING

Pick any Bible verse you like or have had on your mind lately. Write to God every single thought or impression you have about the verse, as if you're talking to your best friend. Be completely honest (it's not like he's fooled), and also include every emotion you have about it.

Then sit back and listen. Open all the entryways into your *hearing* state: feel, sense, know, look for clues, see pictures in your mind. Write it all down.

Underline everything that was kind, good, wise, or thoughtful.

Congratulations! You've just created a personal e-mail from God. If any of it surprises you, write him another letter about your reaction to it and wait again to write down his response.

SURPRISES

What song jumps into your mind right now? Look up the lyrics and see if there's a message for you in them.

What Bible verse springs to mind? What's its message?

What's been annoying you lately? What might God be saying through that irritation?

What was the last thing you ate? What does God think about good food?

When you think of your mode of transportation this week, what's God's perspective on it?

Think of all the people who smiled or laughed with you today. How does God see them?

Think of everyone you had a good conversation with over the last week. Did God speak through them?

What has touched your heart this week? Was God involved?

Notes

See and Know

Notes

REVELATION

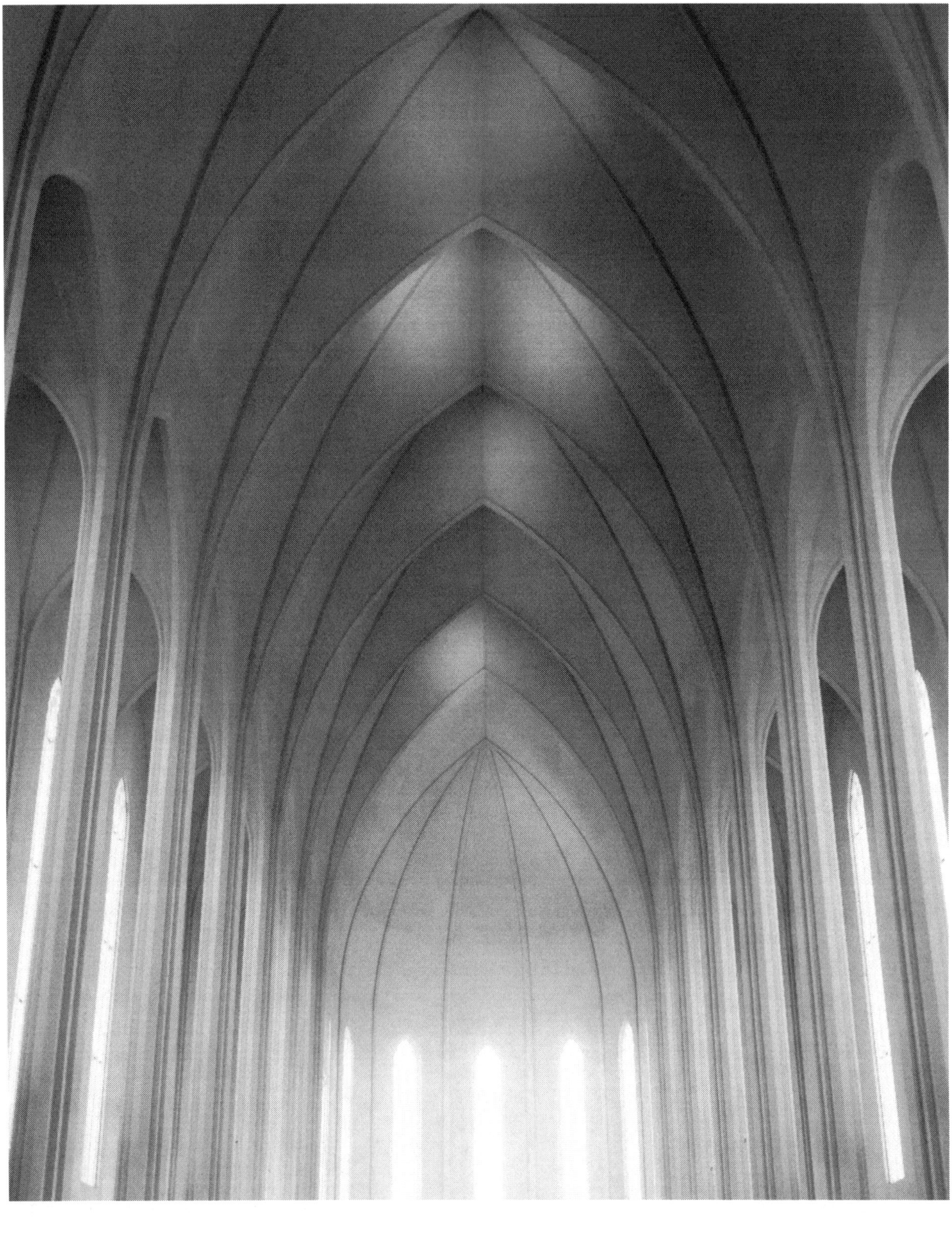

Visions and Dreams

My husband was on drugs and adulterous, and I contracted an STD. I was so sad, especially since I was trusting God and was faithful to my husband. I cried out to God, "Am I not close enough to touch the hem of your garment?" Then I had a vision of coming up behind Jesus and reaching for the hem of his garment. Not only did I touch it, but I put my face in it and wept. He turned and put his hand on my head. When I went back to the doctor, I discovered I was healed with no trace of trouble.

~ Crista

I've had two dreams that stand out to me: One was about French braiding hair, which I couldn't do, but when I woke up, I was a French braid master. The second had to do with solving a differential equation in college. I couldn't, and then I could. I think that each time, I was stuck on something that was within my skill set to solve. I was subconsciously blocked from the answer during my waking hours, but when I dreamed about the solution, I'd remember the dream clearly the next day and could do it.

~ Dona

I had a dream when I was five that put everything in context for me. In it, I was with a host of pastel-colored rainbow souls flying over the earth. We came from a cloud that had the most beautiful music in it, and I knew it was heaven. Each of us was guided by angels, but instead of looking like humans, the angels felt like beams of light with wings. The souls on the earth were brownish and in much pain. We came to help them, comfort them, and in some cases, lift them up to the angels who'd carry them to heaven.

Then I found myself in the body of a little girl. The overwhelming feeling was that it was just my turn. My angels (I had two) left me and flew away back to heaven. I cried and cried because I did not want them to go. I tried to follow them but could no longer fly. I could hear the music coming from heaven and it just made me cry harder because I knew I wouldn't hear it again. Strangely enough, I did when I was nine, and I had to ask it to stop; I just couldn't handle it. I remember thinking that's why babies cry—they see their angels leave them.

~ Tracey

A vision or dream is something that isn't seen with ordinary sight or the rational eye; it's something supernatural or imagined. God said many more people would start having them as the days advanced: "Your young men shall see visions, and your old men shall dream dreams" (Acts 2:17), so we should be experiencing far more in our day.

Psychologists say that we are most often "eye-minded," that is, when we're awake, we're likely to think, imagine, and remember in terms of vision. Naturally, our dreaming is also predominantly visual. Since God created us this way, it's not hard to see why he would choose it as a way to communicate with us.

> *Dreams or visions are mentioned 224 times in the Bible. Abraham, Moses, Jacob, David, Isaiah, Joseph, Jesus, and Paul were all men of action, and their work was helped and not hindered by the dreams and visions sent their way. Paul was an intelligent, knowledgeable, and compelling speaker and leader, and he used analogies and stories to teach. He also embraced the visions and trances that directed his ministry decisions and blessed the church. He knew the power of a picture. While no daydreamer, he recognized the incredible value of heaven-sent dreams.*

God has always talked to his children in dreams, and he still does, but apart from those in the New Age movement, our culture doesn't exactly value them these days. Some assume that dreams and visions are the result of an overactive imagination, and some Christians are afraid of trying to interpret a dream in case God wasn't the one who sent it (perhaps because they are more used to the devil using their imaginations than God, and if they attribute any dream to God, they might be "imagining things").

> *God forbid that he would use something as worldly as the imagination he gave us.*

If you think back to the beginning of the world, God must have had creation all planned out in his head before he spoke it into being. Even when it comes to designing each unique individual, I imagine the Trinity sits together to come up with every aspect of our personality, gifts, and passions. So why wouldn't God use one of his favorite things to speak to us? Why wouldn't he use our creative imaginations to reveal amazing things? How else do you think inventors come up with their ideas, or engineers with their solutions, or choreographers with their dances? *Everything* we enjoy in this world stems from creativity, which begins in the imagination.

We encourage our kids to imagine, but as soon as they get older, suddenly it's not cute and we tell them to stop daydreaming and get serious. When you're younger, you keep going deeper with your imagination, but you don't have to stop as you get older. It's another language God can talk to you with.

Some would say God uses dreams because he has to wait until you're just a little knocked out so you'll finally listen. Some say your thoughts create such a wall of white noise that you can't hear God until they quieten down a bit. Either way, there's probably a message in there for you or someone else. Dreams can:

> **Show us** a direction to take in life
>
> **Warn us** about impending accidents or circumstances
>
> **Show us** what God wants to give us to help us in life
>
> **Warn us** about people's intentions or reveal what's really going on
>
> **Show us** what's going on in someone's life so we can pray
>
> **Encourage or** inspire us
>
> **Show us** how our current choices or actions are affecting others

Some dreams are the asparagus from the night before, some are loosely based on circumstances from our day, and others are not encouraging at all. We can learn to discern the origin of a dream by simply asking God if it's from him or not.

About ten years ago, I dreamed I was wandering through a hospital holding a baby close to my chest. I had given birth, but I didn't feel as if it was my baby because she didn't look like me. "Is this your baby?" I asked one woman after another., holding out the bundle of pink warmth, hoping for a face to light up and arms to reach out. Not one hand stretched out for her. Finally, I stopped to look into her face. There was such understanding there. "It's all right," she said, "I understand what you are doing." I held her until I couldn't let go. "Anna Grace, I will keep you," I murmured. Within two months of this dream, the middle school group at church needed a teacher. I ended up staying in that role for a few years. Interestingly, the name Anna means grace, and God gave me the grace to guide them that entire time.

Additionally, let's not discard a bad dream; even nightmares can tell us a lot. If the enemy is trying to make us afraid of something, the opposite is probably true about us. For example, in a dream where you look stupid, the devil is afraid of you realizing the wisdom and knowledge you have. He wants fear to control you, hence the nightmare. Similarly, you might have a recurring dream of being chased by some unknown horrific creature, and you wake up whenever he catches up with you. To me, that would mean that no matter what makes me scared in life, and no matter what I end up having to come face to face with, I'll always "wake up" and have what I need to get through the reality of the pain. Fear is an emotion we mostly add to the unknowns in life, not the current realities, because when we're right in the middle of something bad, we have God's presence and comfort to make it doable.

I started to keep a notebook by my bed with the goal of writing down every single dream I had. Most nights I couldn't bring myself to wake up enough to do it, and other nights I deluded myself into thinking I'd remember a vivid dream in the morning. Nope. I compromised. I bought a voice recorder and spoke some very groggy and gibberish-like words into it whenever I could.

Once I had that down, I found a favorite dream dictionary online, and I also joined a group of other dream interpreter wannabes. I was a part of that group for about two years (seems to be the amount of time it takes me to learn anything that becomes intrinsic), and here's what I came to realize:

Hearing God can never be reduced to a formula.

Symbols and colors and feelings are all very helpful clues when it comes to interpreting a dream's meaning, but just like God's infatuation with the heart, it all comes down to the heart of the message. You can't interpret God's heart in a dream unless you are intimately connected with it.

The Holy Spirit is the one who reveals the secrets of God. It's up to us to listen and then work with him to get to the root meaning of a dream. So if you dreamed of a brown lake with a dog swimming in it, I would first jump to the dream dictionary to see what those symbols mean, but then I'd ask you what they mean *to you*. An assumptive interpreter (and I use that word loosely) might tell you that brown is the color of poop and that dogs are a man's best friend, so the dream means that your best friend is swimming in poop right now and needs your prayers. But to you, brown is your favorite color in the fall, and you were bitten by a dog as a child, so you have had a morbid fear of them ever since, and lakes make you think of your favorite place to sit. So your dream could actually mean that your greatest fears are coming to an end (fall season) and you don't need to be afraid.

What do you do with your dreams once you figure out what they mean?

Impending circumstances: If you see something negative, ask God what he wants you to pray for, rather than just agreeing with it. In Jeremiah 1, Jeremiah 24, and Amos 7, God gave Jeremiah and Amos visions of upcoming judgments. Amos asked God not to judge Israel as God had shown him he would, and God changed his mind.

Direction: Recognize when your opportunity comes.

Conviction: Repent and quit whatever it is you're doing that doesn't show love to yourself or others.

Visions and trances are sometimes considerably more direct and in your face than dreams, because you're awake when they happen. One goal of visions is revelation for immediate direction, while another deals with the development of the kingdom of God and is for the future. Vision is naturally associated with revivals of religion, and the absence of visions is a sign of spiritual decline (see Lamentations 2:9 and Micah 3:6). The more dreams you have, the greater is the level of spiritual revival in your region.

If you fall into a trance or have a vision, it's highly likely that there's something immediate for you to do with the information you get from it.

- Paul's trance led him to Cornelius's house, and thus began the spread of the gospel to the Gentiles (see Acts 10).
- Joshua's vision gave him the strength and direction he needed to lead the Israelite army into the Promised Land (see Zechariah 3).
- Daniel saw loads of angels and Jesus himself. His visions are the ones that most end-times prophets look at to understand what's happening in the world (most of the book of Daniel).
- Saul had a vision. Ironically, he was blinded, and it led to his changing of history (see Acts 9).
- God appeared to Ananias in a vision with directions to the house where Saul was staying. God wanted him to pray for Saul and restore his sight (see Acts 9:10-19). God must have known he'd have to do something a bit more dramatic to get Ananias over there, given Saul's previous work history, and he figured speaking to him directly might just work.

Always value your dreams and visions and take them to God for interpretation.

TRUTH

What is the truth about our ability to hear God through dreams and trances? Mull over the following Scriptures and write down anything God shows you through them.

"And God spoke to Israel in visions of the night and said, 'Jacob, Jacob.' And he said, 'Here I am.'" (Genesis 46:2).

"And it shall come to pass afterward, that I will pour out my Spirit on all flesh; your sons and your daughters shall prophesy, your old men shall dream dreams, and your young men shall see visions" (Joel 2:28).

"When I had returned to Jerusalem and was praying in the temple, I fell into a trance and saw him saying to me, 'Make haste and get out of Jerusalem quickly, because they will not accept your testimony about me'" (Revelation 2:29).

"And the king said to them, 'I had a dream, and my spirit is troubled to know the dream'" (Daniel 2:3).

"Tell me the interpretation, because all the wise men of my kingdom are not able to make known to me the interpretation, but you are able, for the spirit of the holy gods is in you" (Daniel 4:18).

FINISH THESE SENTENCES

I think dreams and trances are

I want/don't want to let God give me dreams or trances because

I would love to develop my ability to interpret dreams because

When I think about having ongoing trances with God, I

I think I might have misinterpreted my dreams in the past because

For the next few days I'm going to start paying more attention to

DREAM INTERPRETATION

Think of a memorable dream you have had. (If you don't remember one, ask a friend for one of his of hers.)

Are you in the dream or watching?

What's the predominant emotion you have in the dream?

Are there particular colors or objects in the dream that stand out?

Were any words spoken or numbers seen?

Were there any specific or vivid moments?

Is the dream to do with something that happened in the past?

Does the dream feel real or related to real life?

Do you have a *knowing* or sense of the dream's message?

POINTERS

Usually if you are watching the dream, it means you are to pray for the people or circumstances in it.

The emotion can highlight your fears or hopes—emotions you may have squashed during the day. The Holy Spirit is trying to tell you otherwise while you sleep.

Do those colors or objects hold any personal meaning for you? Do you have a dream dictionary you could look up for suggestions?

Words spoken or numbers seen in a dream might hold clues to the dream's interpretation. Look up the etymology of the words (Google "online etymology dictionary"). Look up Bible verses that mention those numbers. Try Strong's Concordance (Google "Strong's numbers") or search "the meaning of numbers in Scripture" on sites that are safe. These can point out things to encourage you or highlight things you can pray about.

Many times unpleasant dreams of past memories show that you need to heal from them.

If it's based on the movie you just watched or book you finished recently, it's probably your creative brain enjoying the sparks.

Think it through, write down your thoughts, and then listen for God's input.

If you notice, every dream can be an expression of God's love. He asks you to pray so his love can shine. He tells you about a good opportunity in advance so you won't miss it. He points out behavior that is pulling you away from your relationship with him or others. He cares about you very much, so listen up when you dream something memorable and write down the details. You never know how it could change a life. Okay, so maybe it won't be as dramatic as the angel telling Mary and Joseph to get out of Egypt, but still, the message is important.

NOTES

VISIONS
AND
DREAMS

Notes

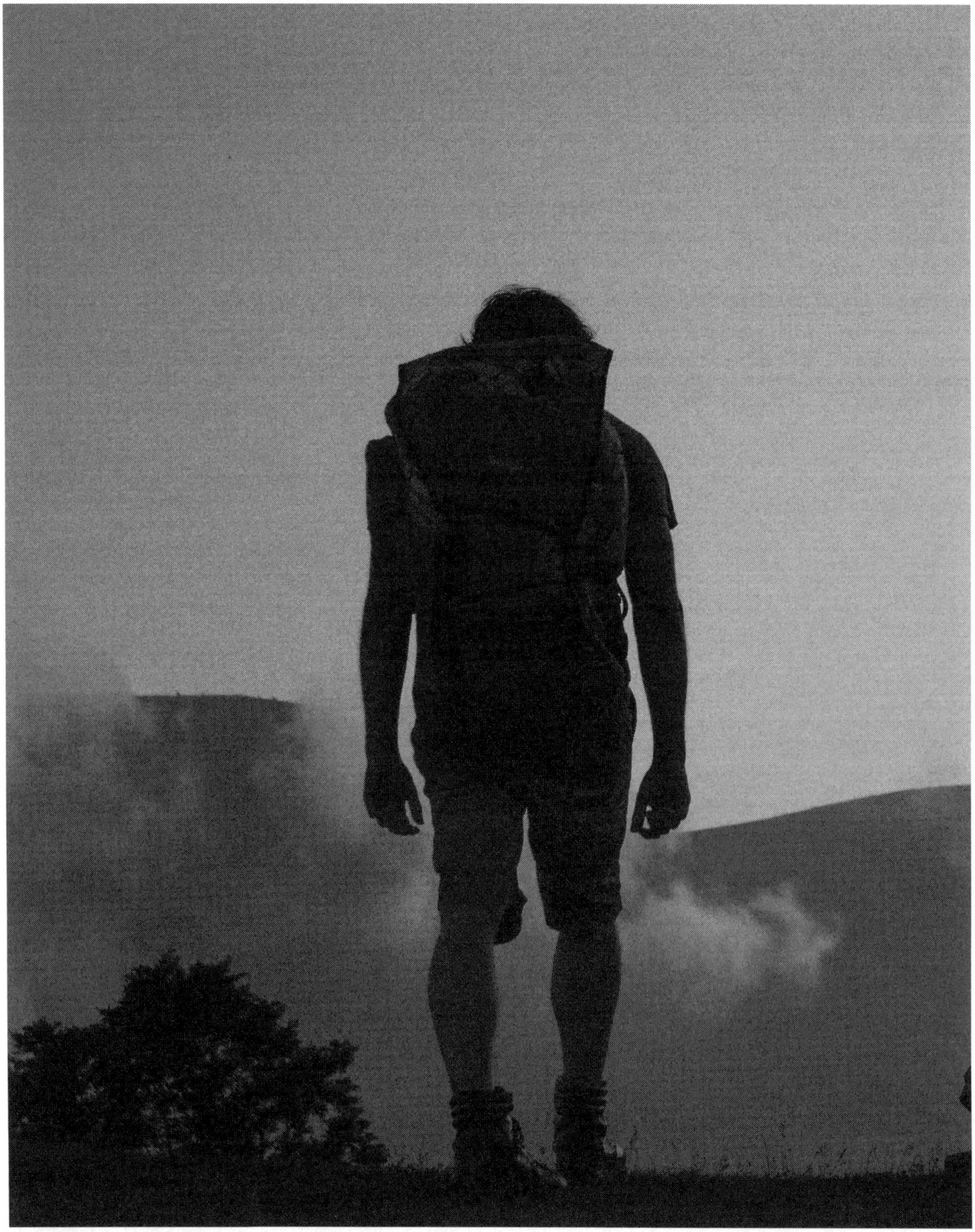

PROPHECY

I was scrolling through Facebook one afternoon, when one of my friends seemed to stand out on the page. I stopped and thought about him for a minute. A lot of the time, I'll see nature images or pictures of particular things like books for people, but this time I saw him lying listlessly on his couch. I felt as if he'd given up trying to make things happen, but at the same time as seeing this picture, I "knew" that he was meant to get back up again and live. I shared my impressions with him. Many months later, I asked him if it had been at all helpful or relevant, and he said that it had been very relevant to things going on in his life at that time and that my "picture" was helpful. Along with other things God had been telling him, it inspired him to find the life in his life.

~ Jean

I was struggling with a leadership position I was in. That night a lady from church called me and let me know that I was the one for the job and I didn't have to know everything to lead. She didn't know I had been feeling discouraged! So it was an encouragement and a confirmation.

~ Heather

I had left my old job with a "call" to do the same thing, but for a church. I had no prospects, just the desire. I was starting to stress after a little while, and a friend told me not to worry, that the job would find me. And it did! A neighbor knocked on my door with the local paper and an ad circled. I was hired within the week.

~ Cathy

I hear God primarily through an inner voice, word, or phrase that, if responded to (pay attention; ask questions; follow insights from Scripture), leads to further dialogue that results in revelation from the Father. There is an inward "knowing" that it's God and not me once it comes, probably because I know his ways and thoughts are not my usual ways or thoughts, and I'm surprised by it.

~ Dennis

Prophecy is God's heart shared with his people through his people. Prophecy is one of the gifts God gives us so we can serve each other well. Check out 1 Corinthians 4:6 in four different translations (emphasis mine):

"What good will I be to you, unless I bring you some revelation or knowledge or prophecy or word of instruction?" (NIV). "If I bring you a revelation or some special knowledge or prophecy or teaching, *that will be helpful"* (NLT). *"How will I benefit you* unless I bring you some revelation or knowledge or prophecy or teaching?" (ESV). *"What will I profit you* unless I speak to you either by way of revelation or of knowledge or of prophecy or of teaching?" (NASB).

So how do we benefit or help people with prophecy? We get to encourage, comfort, confirm, exhort, and inspire. "As each has received a gift, use it to serve one another, as good stewards of God's varied grace" (1 Peter 4:10).

PROPHECY IS NOT ABOUT:

Exposing someone's sin in front of a group of friends—a public shaming

Giving yourself a platform so everyone can look up to you

Having a ministry that implies you're so in touch with God that you don't need family

Sharing the problem without the solution

Calling out people on all the things they do that annoy you. To exhort actually means "to draw near," so when you exhort someone, you have the privilege of calling that person closer to the heart of God.

PROPHECY IS ABOUT:

Calling out the greatness in people and reminding them of how awesomely unique they are

Reminding people that God knows exactly what's going on (good or bad) and that he cares deeply

Confirming things God has already shared with people

Confirming the dreams in people's hearts and encouraging them to move toward their fulfillment

Seeing into people's futures and affirming their hope

Sharing solutions and answers

The closer you get to knowing God and his voice, the better you are at serving that up to benefit others. Perhaps you're afraid of prophecy because you've seen a lot more bad examples than good ones, but that doesn't mean you have to keep it for the prayer closet. It just means you need some practice giving and receiving words in a safe environment. That way you can see up front how a healthy model works and serve from that place of maturity.

We prophesy from identity, not for one.
~ Ben Armstrong

Prophecy is fun! We get to share the heart of God with many people and change lives because of our willingness to share what we hear. Even yesterday I was able to give a girl a word (a prophetic word) based on her phone cover art, and she was in tears over the three main points I told her: Keep moving toward your goal, you don't need to be afraid of it; you have a valid voice, don't be afraid to use it; you've taken up a lot of things and it's time to drop one of them so you can focus on what you're meant to do. It turned out she had a dream of creating jewelry pieces and selling them at fairs, but fear got in the way. The word helped her to know that God cared about her dreams, and he also wanted to encourage her and validate her desire to do something she loved on a bigger scale.

Giving words should never be reserved solely for church. It's always a good time to share God's heart with people! When you live in the moment and in the God zone all the time, you catch those seconds of heaven telling you to go speak to someone or ask a certain question. Moses walked straight past the burning bush, but he didn't hear God speak until he turned toward it, looked, and listened. In the same way, we can walk past a lot of people who need to know God cares without our being available in the Spirit zone. Now don't go beating yourself up about it. It takes practice, but don't miss out on how much of an adventure it is either. God is always speaking, and when you get to be the one he speaks through, life is fuller.

I was in Whole Foods one evening hovering around the chocolate booth (don't judge), and when the girl walked up to help us, I almost missed a sudden flash of light in the corner of my vision. I stopped to think about the girl in front of me and instantly *saw* her painting. I asked her if she painted watercolors and if she loved painting flowers. She was amazed and asked how I knew. I told her I'd been taking a class on how to hear God better (no lie, I take it every day), and that I felt God wanted to encourage her to paint more because it was part of what she was designed to do. She said she hadn't been painting for a while and had just been talking to her mother that weekend about taking it up again. I was able to let her know that she was just as good at hearing God as I was, because all I did was confirm what she'd heard. The conversation ended with her talking about possibly finding a regular church again after years of absence. And the whole thing started with me drooling over chocolate. Validated!

Prophecy is not about telling you what to do as much as it is awakening who you are. ~ Ray Hughes

PROPHECY

"Pursue love, and earnestly desire the spiritual gifts, especially that you may prophesy" (1 Corinthians 14:1). Why does Paul love prophecy so much? Because it makes people happy. Who wouldn't be happy to know that our busy, omnipotent God is looking at them and letting them know how much he loves all the details of their lives?

Except for one memory I have ... many years ago I was praying for a family friend, a former Navy Seal, and God gave me a vision for him. I saw him hitting his wife, shouting at his daughter, and then going to the cliffs to watch for the inevitable invaders sailing toward the shore. The word that came with it was that there was nothing to fear, nothing bad was coming. I shared the word with my pastor and then with the man. Through me, God tried to step in and reassure him, to offer help, to expose the darkness so he could receive some light. But sadly, shortly thereafter, he shot his wife and child and then himself. The only takeaway I have from that time is that God will step in however he can through his people, but it's not always guaranteed to encourage and inspire its recipient.

If you want to be able to prophesy to people, all it takes is a willingness to express what God is sharing. It's scary. I get it, but if you compare the feeling of sharing to the feeling of walking away without having done so, the sharing wins every time. Not many things feel worse than a missed opportunity.

"For you can all prophesy one by one, so that all may learn and all be encouraged" (1 Corinthians 14:31). Apart from the few prophets who are like walking fact knowers, we can *all* prophesy. We can *all* hear God's voice and we can *all* share his heart with others in a way that will teach them something and encourage them. Even for the chosen few (prophets who instantly know many pertinent facts about your life), the office of a prophet is a life calling *for the equipping of the saints to do the works of service"* (1

Corinthians 14:31). We're all on the same page! Isn't it interesting that most of the great verses we have on prophecy are in the love book? We're all in the love chapters. We all get to serve in love. "So, my brothers, earnestly desire to prophesy" (1 Corinthians 14:39).

God often specifically chooses you to be the one to share his words because he likes the way you're going to say them. The more you practice, the more helpful your words will be. The more you practice, the greater you'll trust that God knows what he's doing by using you as his mouthpiece. "Having gifts that differ according to the grace given to us, let us use them: if prophecy, in proportion to our faith" (Romans 12:6). I've been practicing for a long, long time, mainly because it's extremely rewarding to push people closer to God and into his heart. It was people's stories that first inspired me to try it out, so I had a very helpful group of friends let me practice on them and vice versa. When I was stuck at home with two small children and no car, I'd go through the church phone list and call people I felt led to pray specific things over. Being able to encourage them was great, and the more I practiced hearing and sharing, the more of a blessing (I was told) I became.

Shawn Bolz, in his amazing book *Translating God*, recounted this:

> When I lived in Kansas City, we would deliberately share rides with lots of people from our local church and practice the prophetic in the car. One way we would practice is by praying for friends and family that we knew but the others in the car didn't. They would try to hear God about our relatives and then ask questions to see if they heard right. "Is it a woman in her thirties? Is it an older man? Are they starting new jobs?" It sounded like twenty questions at first, because we were all just trying to hear God together and were practicing in a safe place. We would all get a ton of things wrong. Even I, leading these times, got so many pieces of information wrong … but then something shifted. God honored our hunger and we started to get great accuracy. We learned in those times to feel the difference between our thoughts and God's. We would feel the different weight on some of our impressions versus others that we were emotionally attached to.

Some people have been very fond of using their ability to hear God to manipulate others. "You're going to marry me." "You're going to start crocheting booty shorts and giving me 50 percent of the proceeds." "You're going to apologize to me and then voluntarily resign." All sad but true … although I might have made up the one about the booty shorts. A woman called me one time to ask me about the latest thing her husband was asking her to do. She had told him no, so his response was that he'd then prophesy it to her and she'd have to do it. I suggested that he go to the pastor with his "prophecy" to see what the pastor thought about the word and the obedience of the man's wife. That went down like a lead balloon. Don't turn advice or control into a word. It's manipulative and it's witchcraft.

Let your words be judged. Expect the word to be examined.

Others seem to think their words are only good for leadership. They have a "gift" of pointing out the bad things they notice about how the church is run, so they feel obliged to share. Below are some questions you can ask yourself before you decide to share your word.

CHECKLIST FOR ALL WORDS

Do I have a naturally judgmental perspective on life? Is this word one of those judgments?

Am I giving this word so leadership or people will notice me and think I'm important?

Do I have an agenda in giving this word?

Do any of the leaders or people actually know me as a friend? Have I spent time getting to know them before going in to deliver my truth bombs?

Am I willing to have this word examined and possibly rejected?

Can I deliver this word in a humble way?

Will I get offended if this word is rejected?

As you can tell, there is a high need to know your heart before delivering a word. If there's anything in it for *you*, it's probably not time to give them a word. It's probably more to do with an issue in your own heart. If you still feel the need to share it, and you truly believe the word will benefit and bless them, do so and then go home and ask God if you have any more responsibility with it. Once God says your responsibility is lifted, don't worry about it anymore.

If you're having a rough time with negative thoughts, work with God on cultivating your own atmosphere of peace, love, hope, and joy. The more time you spend in God's presence and the more you filter the words that come out of your mouth, the better your personal atmosphere will become. Light is stronger than darkness! The more intensely good your atmosphere gets, the wider the influence you'll have and the more you can affect others for the good, as Terri got to do recently:

"Today we were boarding a plane to Los Angeles, and the attendant at the door said, 'Have a good day' on our way in. I asked him how he was doing and he said, 'Good.' Immediately, I felt the Spirit all over me and a little like I was slipping through the floor of the plane. I knew he was having a very hard day, so after a little squeal from the instant whack, I turned and told him it was going to get better. He asked if it would get better for him or for me. I told him better for him, and better and better. He said he hoped so. When we exited the plane, he was much happier."

Ministering God's gifts from a place of love can be a scary thing, but the joy in doing so is so worth it. During a season of offering to pray for every homeless person I met, I stopped at the lights one day and rolled down the window for one. I asked him if there was anything I could pray for, and he said he had heart problems. I prayed a quick prayer and asked if he felt anything around his heart area, and he said (and this still makes me tear up), "No, but it sure was nice to hold your hand." Even if all you feel you can give is a touch, you can still help someone feel loved and that he or she matters.

And in order to love well, you need to let others love *you,* which means you have to become vulnerable and let down the drawbridge. It means you have to let people see the real you. It means people might start letting you see the real them. Living with open hearts—your own and those of others—is a big responsibility, but it has to be done. You can walk into a church and light up the place with prophetic words and healings, and walk out of there just as alone as when you walked in. Oh, to be sure, you'll have had a lot of people clamoring for special one-on-one time with you so they can get a word or a healing, but your heart needs a home base.

You need a family that loves you, believes in you, inspires you, and is with you when you celebrate or mourn or are afraid. Yes, flow with every single gift of the Spirit, but do it from that base, that place of love. If you're feeling loveless, stick with his people. You may have a lot of pain, walls, and judgments in that heart of yours, but you'll eventually find some good eggs. Their love will win you over and turn your heart into that ball of mush you've been afraid of letting it become since kindergarten. Trust me, it's not so bad.

Being deeply loved by someone gives you strength, while loving someone deeply gives you courage.
~ Lao Tzu

TRUTH

What is the truth about prophecy? Mull over the following Scriptures and write down anything God shows you through them.

"For the Lord God does nothing without revealing his secret to his servants the prophets" (Amos 3:7).

"On the other hand, the one who prophesies speaks to people for their upbuilding and encouragement and consolation" (I Corinthians 14:3).

"I will pour out my Spirit on all flesh; your sons and your daughters shall prophesy" (Joel 2:28).

"Pursue love, and earnestly desire the spiritual gifts, especially that you may prophesy" (I Corinthains 14:1).

"Now there are varieties of gifts, but the same Spirit; and there are varieties of service, but the same Lord; and there are varieties of activities, but it is the same God who empowers them all in everyone. To each is given the manifestation of the Spirit for the common good … to another prophecy" (I Corinthians 12:4-7).

FINISH THESE SENTENCES

I think prophecy is

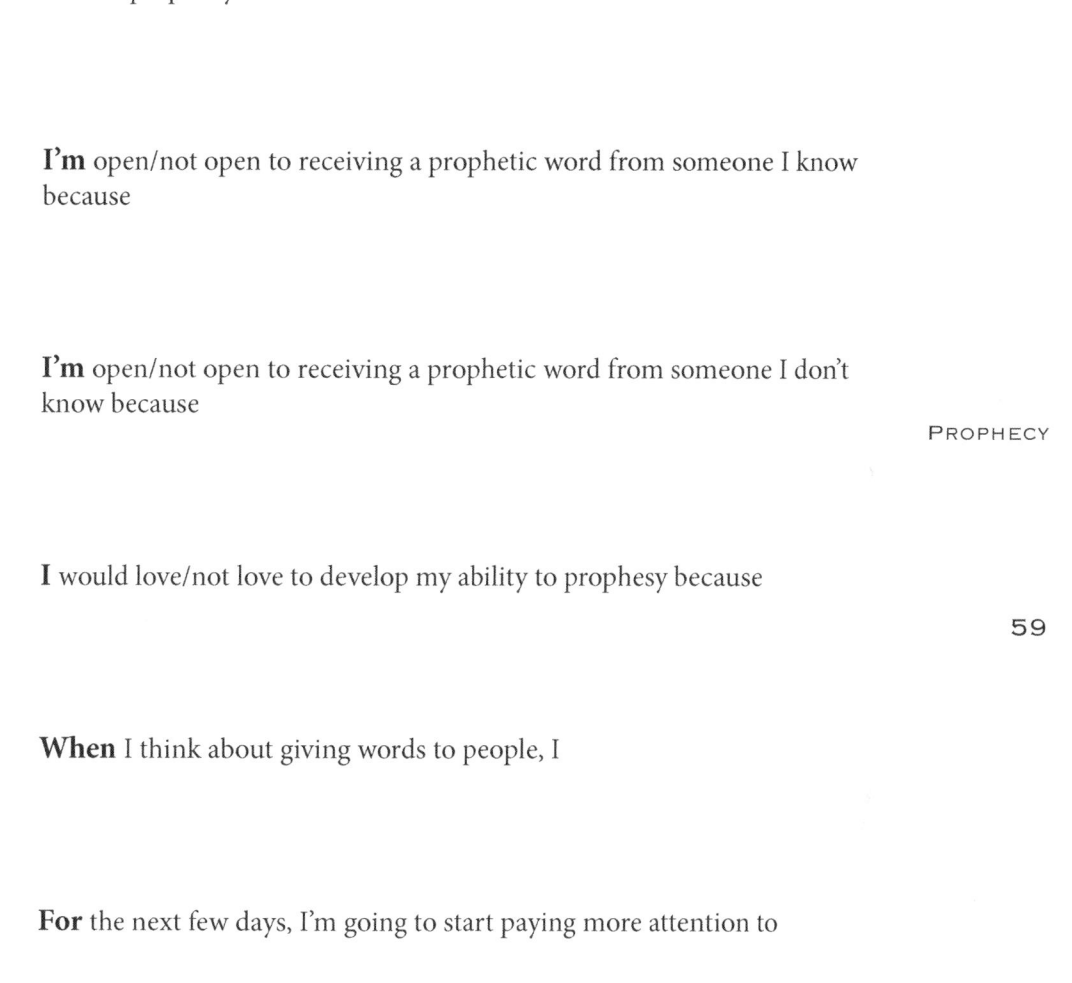

I'm open/not open to receiving a prophetic word from someone I know because

I'm open/not open to receiving a prophetic word from someone I don't know because

I would love/not love to develop my ability to prophesy because

When I think about giving words to people, I

For the next few days, I'm going to start paying more attention to

SHARE A PICTURE

The easiest way to practice the prophetic is with a group of like-minded individuals, but if you have no one nearby, give the words to yourself.

Stand behind a random person in your group.

Close your eyes and focus on the first picture you *see* for that person. Zoom in for more details, as with earlier exercises.

Based on what you see, its function, and the setting it's in, ask God for an interpretation of it.

Ask the person if the picture means anything. Many times you learn more by asking the person *before* you give your own interpretation of it.

Was the word encouraging? Did it benefit the receiver?

Prophecy
SHARE A FOCUSED PICTURE

With your team member in mind, ask God for a picture of a rock or a flower.

Zoom in for the detail, setting, colors, and other items present.

If that picture describes your team member's life right now, ask your team member what God might be saying and then give your own interpretation of it. See how the interpretations match up (or don't).

SHARE A FEELING

Sit in front of someone and see if you can sense the emotion he or she is experiencing—happy, sad, nervous—so you can learn what's from God and what isn't.

Ask if you can take his or her hand and see if you can feel more of what the Spirit wants to share.

If the emotion you feel is postiive, share that by saying, "God wants to give you courage," or "God loves your joy." Don't tell a man it feels like he is in a lousy mood, because even if he isn't, he's guaranteed to be in one after you share that. Turn it into a positive word by looking at his heart instead.

If the emotions you feel are negative, ask if you can pray for anything. Don't say what you're feeling, just approach it with the opposite, positive emotion.

SHARE A *KNOWING*

Move beyond what you see into the heart of God and listen.

Can you *see* or *hear* a word?

Is there a phrase, song lyrics, or random thought coming to mind? Does the name of a movie or book come to mind? Ask God what it might mean.

Do you just *know* something the person needs to hear that will encourage him or her?

Ask the person if your *knowing* or words mean anything.

Pray for the person if he or she wants prayer.

SHARE FROM CLUES

Look at the person's clothing, hair, or shoes for clues.

Ask God to help you tune in to sense or know certain things that you can use to encourage the person. For example, "Your shoes are strong and sturdy. I can see how well God made your heart; you're such a safe place for others to find refuge."

Look around you at other things nearby. For example, a clock might tell you that God is promising to be on time with his direction for the person, or that his love is never ending, or that his promises do not necessarily operate on our timeline.

PRACTICE GETTING WORDS OF KNOWLEDGE

Practice getting birthdates, family names, anniversary dates, and the like.

PRACTICE GIVING PRESENT AND FUTURE WORDS

I find future words harder to perceive, but practice truly does make it easier. I try to track with all my senses to give a word in season that will encourage and bless the receiver (or kick that person into action mode).

NOTES

Prophecy

Notes

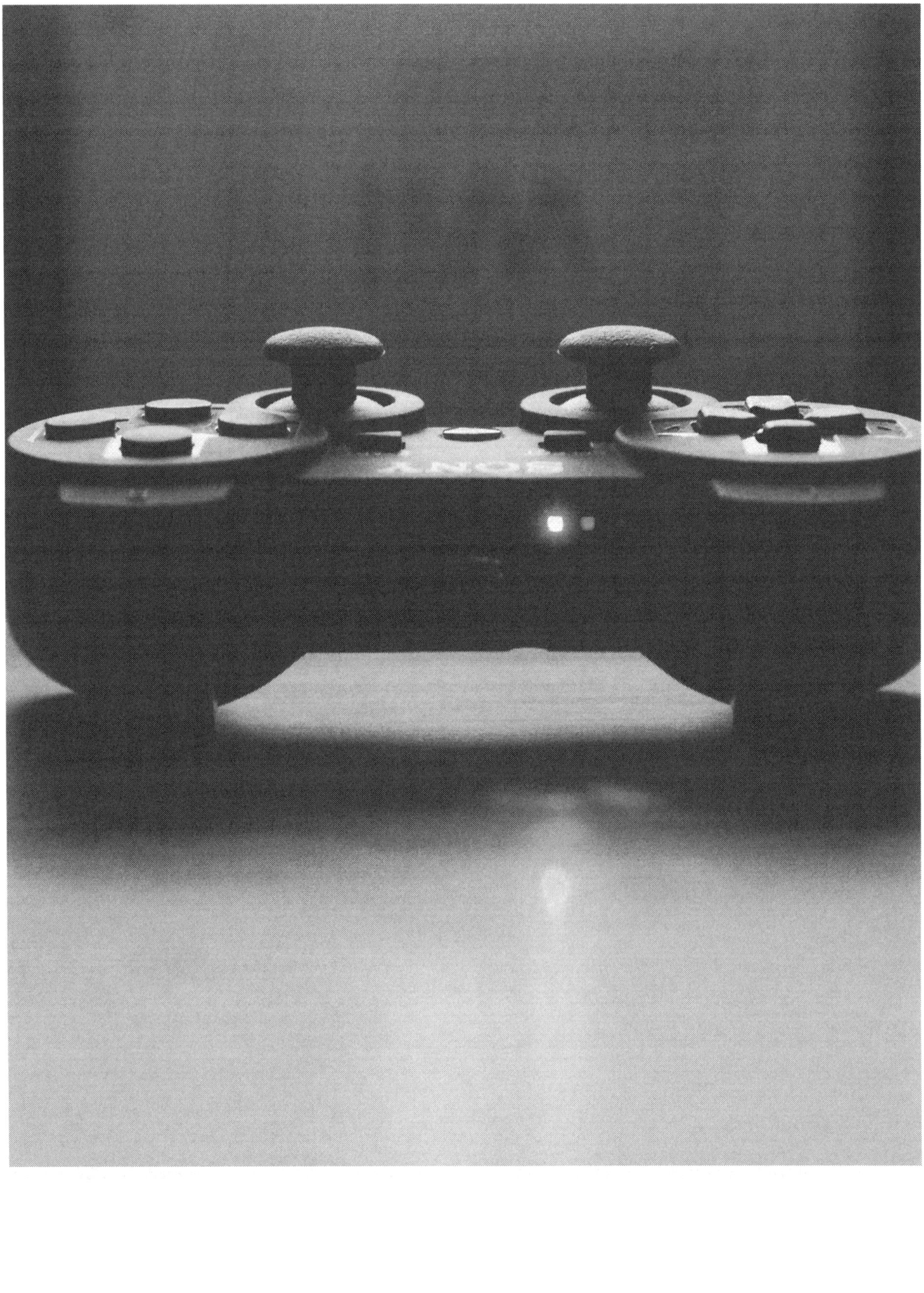

JUDGING PROPHECY

Someone saw my shoes and told me that he thought of the song "Diamonds on the Soles of Her Shoes." He said he felt the Lord was saying I had something really valuable to offer that was hidden. The really cool thing about it was that the song was one of the few songs that Paul Simon did with a group from South Africa called Lady Smith Black Mambazo. They were my absolute favorite band. It felt like a deeply personal message from a person I had only met that day.

~ Aspen

I have a friend who has been in a relationship with the same guy for a couple of years now, and she found herself suddenly attracted to another man she works with. This bothered her, and she was wondering why she felt that way. She mentioned that another girl at work was really attracted to him. I described some of my experience with being a feeler and advised her to talk to God about it and see if it was her own or the other girl's emotion. She came back to me a few days later, having discovered it wasn't hers, and it was completely gone!

~ Rebecca

Several years ago, a minor physical ailment was troubling me. I had tried everything I knew for quite a long while, and yet the problem persisted. Having run out of every option I could find to resolve the issue, I became convinced this was a spiritual battle. I asked trusted friends to pray diligently with me in defeating this demonic attack against my body.

One of my friends mentioned an impression he received when he prayed for me. He sensed that I should stop eating a certain food. Could it be that simple? No demons? No spiritual warfare? Sure enough, I stopped eating that food and the problem disappeared. I was in darkness about what I should do, but one prophetic word shed light on the situation and brought about a healing in my body.

~ Bob Hazlett, *The Roar: God's Sound in a Raging World*

Satan's objective is to persuade us that the person giving us a word is not really hearing God. The value you place on the word determines the power you receive from it, and often the value you place on a word is based on what you think of the person giving it. The more you know about the person, the more you know his heart and his connection with the Father. When you get a word from someone you know well and value, you are more likely to steward the word and let it grow your relationship with God.

Prophecy and words of knowledge accelerate the intensity of God's love. Receiving a word is like having a FaceTime with heaven. It's more real and intimate and personal than a text.
~ Shawn Bolz

JUDGING PROPHECY

How do you know when it's God speaking and not the person giving the word? How do you judge a word well? Lots of words aren't completely accurate in a prophetic culture because most people are growing in their relationship with God and they are still learning how to hear his voice more clearly. Examine everything and keep the good stuff. Early on in people's walks, the words they give will be partly them, partly God, and partly your interpretations. Give them the grace to keep practicing.

PRACTICE

In Malcolm Gladwell's book *Outliers,* he says that the best people with any specific talent are those who have practiced for over 10,000 hours. It's not so much based on talent but on the time given to develop it. That's the equivalent of thirty-eight hours a week for five years. Compare that to a marriage—the amount of time a couple actually spends together is usually nowhere close to thirty-eight hours a week. Twenty years into a marriage, though, that couple will have racked up many more hours together. If you watch couples who have been together that long (who still like each other), you'll notice the closeness of their communication. They understand each other. They know the patterns of their thoughts. They can usually finish the other person's sentences (although I don't recommend it!).

It's the same way with God. The longer we hang out with him and talk and listen, the closer we'll be to his thoughts. We'll know his perspective and we'll be better at sharing his heart with others. We'll also be better able to know which parts of a person's word for us are really God speaking or not.

Do you trash a word just because it isn't confirming something God's already told you? Did you know prophecy doesn't always confirm what God's already said (Samuel, you'll be king—see 1 Samuel 10:1)? We teach it because we're afraid of words that encourage people to do stupid things. We should never avoid encouraging people to share specific words about the future, but we should definitely do a better job of teaching people how to examine a word and keep the good parts.

FEELINGS

It's very easy to base our value of a word on our feelings, especially if the main way we hear God is through those feelings. I can instantly hear some of you say.ing, "Oh no, never, ever trust your feelings. Emotions are so carnal. Go with any other way of hearing God, but not that!" Not true. Some of you are particularly designed to hear God that way. That said, your senses need to be trained to be able to distinguish the difference between God's voice and your thoughts.

Many Christians have given words according to what they thought was their discernment, but it was really based on a feeling they had about a person and they added their own words to it. I'll confess, back when I was a new Christian, I gave a woman a word one time about not needing to read her poetry from the church stage as if it were a word from God. Truth be told, I was just irritated at her lack of talent and wanted her to stop. People will do that. Maybe the first time they met a certain leader, they were offended because the leader gave them "a look," not understanding that their own unhealed issues of rejection had caused them to read that leader wrong.

Hebrews 5 talks about mature Christians having their senses trained for discernment.

This can have to do with either your five bodily senses or the understanding of your mind. It is actually extremely common to feel other people's emotions. For example, can you think of a time when you walked into a room and suddenly felt different than you did before you entered? That feeling is most commonly called discernment, and it can be used to discern good and evil. Some pick up on sexual sin easily, some pick up on people's negative emotions, and some even feel other people's physical pain. This is rarely talked about in the church, so most people are very hesitant to share their experiences in this area. Many people have been marked as crazy because it doesn't make sense to feel what others are feeling, especially when the people whose emotions they are picking up on appear fine. What can happen when you relate this to prophecy, though, is that you can pick up on what's going on in people and allow it to nullify the word they're giving you. Alternatively, your emotional wounds can be triggered, and in your state of prophetic immaturity, you translate that to mean that the person giving the word has your problems! Or you could be giving someone a word and prophesy your own problems over him because they feel like his.

As you grow in discernment, you'll come to know which feeling means what, and you'll come more and more into the knowledge of what God's truth feels like as opposed to someone else's emotional state.

START BY JUDGING THE WORD.

Getting prophetic words is generally a great, feel-good experience, but if you do nothing with them, they may easily end up as words on an old recording or piece of paper. "Do not quench the Spirit. Do not despise prophetic utterances, but examine everything carefully, hold fast to that which is good" (1 Thessalonians 5:19-21). What do you do with a word?

- Is it a word of knowledge, a word for now, or a word for the future? It's possible to get a word that's scriptural but it's not what God is saying to you right now.
- Does it sit well with your spirit? It's possible to get a word that is partially true, because people are always practicing. "For we know in part and we prophesy in part" (1 Corinthians 13:9). When perceiving, people can make mistakes.
- Does it line up with Scripture and the heart of God? Does this word bring you closer to God and his people?
- Can the Holy Spirit say yes and amen to it? Flush what's bad. It's not your job to receive something just because someone thinks he's hearing from God. If the word is off, don't receive it.
- If the word seems way off, but it bothers you and you can't trash it, ask the prophets and leadership if they are in agreement with the word, the interpretation, and its application.

THE INTERPRETATION MUST BE GOD'S, NOT YOURS.

You need the Holy Spirit's anointing. Take the word home with you and talk it out with God. Again, go deeper and ask him if there's more he wants to say. Ask him what opportunities you have right now to step into those words.

For example, if you want to be a writer, you start by being a writer today, not when someone else recognizes you as one.

STEWARD YOUR WORDS AND PROMISES.

When we're faithful with little, we get more. "And the elders of the Jews built and prospered through the prophesying of Haggai the prophet and Zechariah the son of Iddo" (Ezra 6:14).

TRUST THAT GOD WANTS YOUR DAYS TO FULFILL YOUR DESIGN.

Prophecies must be mixed with faith to come true—only Joshua and Caleb saw the Promised Land. Unbelief can kill a prophecy and keep the purposes of God from happening in your life. He wants us to be involved with him and trust him to see our destinies fulfilled.

KEEP YOUR WORDS AROUND.

It's very common to get something completely new out of your words even a month down the road because you've changed. God's word is alive, and it can speak to you in a new way, wherever you are. Keeping the words will help you see how far you've come. They'll remind you of how you felt when you first received them.

WATCH OUT FOR SELECTIVE HEARING.

You may want to quit your job or travel so badly that you take any word as confirmation when all I've said is that you have pretty hair. Don't make the word fit your level of desperation. Maybe you've been praying for a mate for years and someone gives you a word about companionship. God was talking about adopting a dog, but you automatically turned it into a word about *twue lurve* (*Princess Bride* reference). Don't run after it blindly without asking God and wise people around you for counsel.

TALK TO GOD ABOUT THE WORD IF IT'S UNSETTLING.

Sometimes God wants to see how you respond to a word. He told Moses he was going to kill the Israelites, but he didn't really want to. He was testing Moses's heart.

REMIND GOD OF HIS WORDS.

Jacob wanted all of God and was willing to fight him over a blessing. We never have to fight for a blessing these days; it's fully available to us in the form of God's constant presence and power. Many times God wants us to participate in the unfolding of our words by speaking as if they're going to happen, praying over them, and staying close to his will. "I will give you the keys of the kingdom of heaven, and whatever you bind on earth shall be bound in heaven, and whatever you loose on earth shall be loosed in heaven" (Matthew 16:19).

GIVE FEEDBACK TO THE PERSON WHO GAVE YOU THE WORD.

Assuming most of those who give you words are within your church community, be sure to help them grow by giving them feedback based on the bullet points above, and tell them how their words related to your current season. Feedback will help keep a healthy prophetic church culture of accountability and humility.

I was at a meeting recently to hear a speaker with a prophetic ministry. At the end of his talk, he went around the room and named people's pain points, causing almost all of them to cry. Prophetic ministry is not a gift God gives so you can point out people's pain, it's a gift you use to inspire and encourage. If you're going to be the messenger, then don't publically remind people about the pain they're going through without giving very specific hope and comfort at the end of it. Just because you can see things in the Spirit realm doesn't mean you should broadcast it all. I much prefer those who go around the room and give very short words like, "Things are going to change in the next two weeks for you. It's all going to be brand new and you'll wonder how you ever felt this way." Once, I heard a man receive a word about his prodigal son coming home. When he got home there was a message from that son on his answering machine that led to reconciliation.

Be the giver or harbinger of hope. Be the messenger who inspires and encourages.

ASK GOD ABOUT WHAT TO DO WITH YOUR WORD WHEN IT'S DELAYED.

Abraham wasn't seeing God's promise of a son fulfilled, but instead of asking God what to do, Sarai tried to half-fulfill it by offering him Hagar (read Genesis 16). This resulted in Ishmael, who also received the promise, but the angel said, "He shall be a wild donkey of a man, his hand against everyone and everyone's hand against him, and he shall dwell over against all his kinsmen" (Genesis 16:12). "Helping" God speed things up won't always turn out to be your best decision.

In her book *Heaven Awaits the Bride*—her account of a vision of heaven—Anna Rountree recounted her encounter with an angel of promise, during which she discovered that God had no problem waiting years to fulfill his promises over her life.

She asked the angel if he had been delivering promises on earth, and he told her that he had been delivering hers. She was surprised, and couldn't even remember the Lord's promise to her that she would see into heaven, because it had been twenty years since he'd told her she would.

At first she had longed for its fulfillment, but as the years passed, she forgot his words. God had not forgotten, though, and in his time, he fulfilled his promise. The whole book is filled with her descriptions of what she saw. Everything happens in his perfect time, not in our idea of it.

Even the Bible is full of "delayed" promises.

Samuel anointed David as king of Israel when he was a teenager, but David didn't actually become king until he was thirty (see 2 Samuel 5:3-4).

Thirty years passed before Abraham had his promised son.

The Israelites had to travel for forty years and then fight many battles before the Promised Land became theirs.

Talk of Jesus's presence on earth was mentioned in multiple books of the Old Testament, but Jesus wasn't born until hundreds of years later.

Paul knew he'd get to witness in Rome, but he was stuck in jail for two years in Caesarea, was shipwrecked and almost died, and he stayed on Malta for a spell before he ever got to Rome.

Jesus still hasn't come back.

I'm of the opinion that God's ultimate vision is for us all to know him, and no matter what promises we cling to in the hopes of having them complete us, Jesus is enough for our hearts as we wait.

If you have unfulfilled promises, don't lose your hope. Don't get mad at God. It might just be that God has the perfect time to make that promise happen, and it isn't necessarily today.

TRUTH

What is the truth about judging prophecy? Mull over the following Scriptures and write down anything God shows you through them.

"Behold, I send my messenger before your face, who will prepare your way before you" (Luke 7:27).

"A light for revelation to the Gentiles, and for glory to your people Israel" (Luke 2:32). Does this word bring light and glorify God?

"In their greed they will exploit you with false words" (Joel 2:28). What's the heart behind the message?

"And he will turn many of the children of Israel to the Lord their God" (Luke 1:16). When you prophesy from a place of love, it should lead people toward God.

"Today, if you hear his voice, do not harden your hearts" (Hebrews 4:7).

"Paul stood up among them and said, 'Men, you should have listened to me and not have set sail from Crete and incurred this injury and loss. Yet now I urge you to take heart, for there will be no loss of life among you, but only of the ship'" (Acts 27:18-44).

FINISH THESE SENTENCES

I think judging prophecy is

I value the words I receive from people who

I know how to recognize the Holy Spirit's parts of words by

When I think about giving feedback to people who give me prophetic words, I

I rate my ability to judge a word well as being _____ percent. I think I can grow that by

I steward my words by

JUDGE YOUR WORDS

Is it a word of knowledge, a word for now, or a word for the future?

Am I making this word fit my level of desperation?

Does it sit well with my spirit?

Does it line up with Scripture and the heart of God? Does this word bring me closer to God and his people? Can the Holy Spirit say yes and amen to it?

If it's bothering you, are the prophets or leadership in agreement with the word, the interpretation, and its application?

Does God have more to say about this word?

STEWARD YOUR WORDS

Have I given the person who gave me this word some healthy feedback?

Can I mix this word with my faith to see it fulfilled?

What opportunities do I have right now to step into these words?

Am I willing to wait for God to fulfill this on his timeline, not mine?

I've gone back to review other words I've received in the past and found …

Notes

NOTES

Judging Prophecy

Revolution

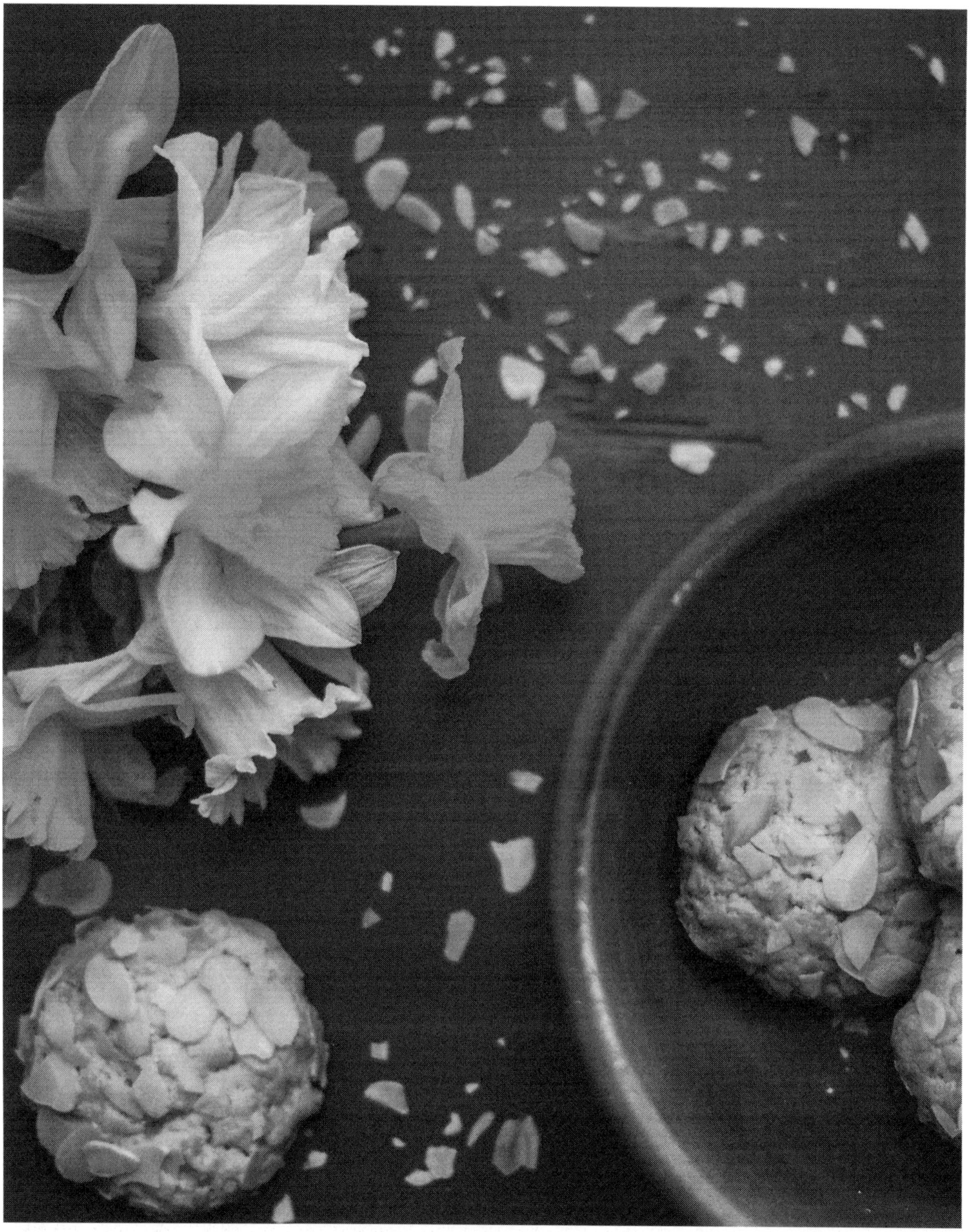

PHYSICAL HEALING 7

Everyone was excited that a woman in our church was miraculously healed of breast cancer, so I asked her prayer team to pray for me. When asked what I needed healing for, I thought of a few things but decided to let God figure it out. (I was a fairly new Holy Spirit-filled believer.) So they all prayed in the Holy Spirit and laid hands on me. I was told to not let the devil steal my healing, although I didn't know what it was until I went to get my checkup by my OB/GYN months later. At my exam he jumped back and exclaimed, "What is this?" It seems I was completely healed of endometriosis.

~ Linda

My son, Christian, was injured in a Friday football game in junior high and taken off the field to the ER with a separated shoulder. The ER doctor ordered X-rays, confirmed it was separated, and said to keep it immobilized in a sling for six to eight weeks. We went to the Friday night youth service, and during praise and worship, God's presence filled the room. Some of the youth began to pray for Christian. He ran to the bathroom to look at his shoulder because he felt God had healed him. He came back in swinging his arm around, saying he was healed and the pain was gone. On Monday we took him to the orthopedic surgeon with the X-rays from the ER. My son told him what happened at church and began to move his arm. The doctor didn't believe him, so he ordered more X-rays. We all stood in awe as the new X-rays showed that his shoulder was completely normal!

~ Sally

When our kids were small, we had a small dachshund named Chamille. She got kicked by a cow and it broke her jaw. I could feel where it was broken. Our five-year-old daughter said, "Mommy, let's pray." Well first I said a little silent prayer that God would not hurt her faith (I didn't have much faith that God would heal a dog). We prayed. The next morning Chamille was eating dry food and her jaw was normal. I will always remember the faith of a child.

~ Dawn

I remember the first time I saw someone healed through me. I was in Paris for a few days to join some friends on a mission trip, and one of the girls on our team badly sprained her ankle. It had swollen up to twice its size and was turning purple. A few of us gathered around her, put our hands on her ankle, and started to pray. I felt her swelling go down under my hand, and when we finished, her ankle looked perfect. She was able to stand and walk just fine.

Up to that time, I'd been praying for people for physical healing for about a year. I'd followed the model I was given and nothing ever happened, but it didn't discourage me enough (which I blame on all the faith-filled books I'd read over the previous ten years).

There's something about hanging out with God that makes you feel like you were born to kill giants.

PHYSICAL HEALING

That ankle healing was the beginning of many. It's difficult to remember them all, but some stand out—the guy with the dislocated knee completely healed and jumping on his leg at the mall, the girl with chronic neck pain healed instantly at a coffee shop, the guy with pain in his foot for a month fully healed by the following morning, the friend who had lost her voice and instantly got it back full force. So much goodness and kindness of heaven on display. It's mind-blowing, and in some ways it's like a drug: you keep wanting to see more people free of pain.

My prayer methods have changed a lot since the '80s, but the premise is the same. I see people in pain. I offer to pray. I either ask them if I can put a hand on their shoulder or get them to do it, or I tell them to take my hand. Regardless, the presence of God in me and around me is released, and they either get healed, or the pain lessens, or they feel the love of God. Many times I'll pray over the phone and see a higher ratio of results, probably because I have more faith for God to show up. Yes, it's awkward and scary to walk up to a stranger or offer a prayer on a social media site, but I figure I'm offering a better life, and my regret would be greater than my awkwardness anyway.

The easiest people to pray for are the unbelievers, and the hardest are the Christians. Why? Because their fear gets in the way of their healing. Some seem to think they'll contract some sort of Pentecostal virus if they let me pray, or they launch into religious mode and do so many strange things—like praying louder than me or saying things that drain any faith or hope out of the moment—that it blocks them from just letting God in to heal whatever it is that's wrong.

Why would you suddenly change everything about your walk with God and start offering to pray for people in, gasp, person? Well …

WHY

> *We're supposed to do everything Jesus did and more, and he spent an awful lot of his time healing the sick. He was always moved by compassion; his heart was always to see people healed and in their right senses; his love led the way (see John 14:12-14).*

If we're to pray the way Jesus said to pray, we're to ask for life on earth to be just like it is in heaven. No one is sick in heaven, no one is in pain, and no one is brokenhearted. Jesus either took all of our sickness onto his body and died with it, never again to resurface, or he didn't. So for the devil to try to insinuate that our pain or sickness is God-sent is ridiculous. To tell you the truth, it really angers me. I just won't agree with it, ever!

We're here to spread the love, spread the goodness and kindness of God, and bring heaven to earth.

We're here to be a conduit for healing to whoever needs it, and the more we do it, the more people will be healed. Now yes, I have seen someone limp by many times and not offered to pray. I wish I had, but I'm not going to beat myself up over those times. I'm going to keep moving forward and never let shame and regret hold me back. Regrets only stay alive if I maintain them.

I'm going to live this Jesus-modeled life whenever I can. For instance: Today I got to pray for a homeless guy's knee and get him lunch. After I got home, I got to pray over the phone for a sweet lady with cancer. The knockout presence of God in my room was incredible, and she reported the same on her end. A few days ago I held a man's hand and asked him if he could feel God's love coming through and reaching his heart. Through his tears, he asked if he could hug me, and we both felt the Holy Spirit minister. This is the way normal life should be! We have everything we need inside us, we just have to be brave and get over ourselves so we can place the healing of another person as a higher priority than our fear.

HOW

But, but … what do I say? How do I say it? I have a few different lines I use, based on what I feel the Holy Spirit is up to. I said to one guy, "This might sound weird, but sometimes when I pray for people, they get healed. Can I pray for your ankle?" And to another girl: "I've been told I have a healing gift and sometimes people get better when I pray for them. Take my hand," and I held it out. Almost everyone has felt the strong presence of God, even when healing doesn't come. Most of them have asked how it works, so I tell them it's God's healing flowing through me to them. I usually add how much he hates seeing them in pain and that he wants them to be pain free.

WHAT

What better way is there to worship than to let God do his thing and give him the glory for it? Every healing, every bit of peace, every heart healed, every bit of opportunity we get to show God off through flowing with him is so *good!* You don't need to organize special times and days to go out to pray for people. You just need to get in the God zone and live there, because we reflect the nature of the world we allow ourselves to be most aware of—earth or heaven. His presence is sweet, he's always talking and leading the way, and you get to live this life fully alive. You get to carry heaven and plonk it down in front of people and say, "Here, have a bite. Doesn't that taste so good? Here, have some more, and more, and more, and more." When we're full of the Holy Spirit, we're always readymade and ready to pour.

> *The most outstanding feature of Kuhlman's ministry was her insistence on absolute dependence on the Holy Spirit. This emphasis appears to have been unique among those with healing ministries. No one before Kuhlman had highlighted the importance of the role the Holy Spirit played in healing to the degree to which she did.*
> ~ Dictionary of Pentecostal Charismatic Movements

A lot of Christians I know are drawn toward the fire aspect of the Holy Spirit. They crave the excitement and rush of a new miracle, a powerful testimony, and the opportunity of visibility if it occurs through them. Doing things out of desire for attention is not love. Doing things for the adrenaline rush is not love. So how can we balance going into all the world with our selfish reasons for doing so?

I don't think you need to worry. As I mentioned before, life is an adventure. You're not going to turn into Mother Theresa the second you get saved. God knows your heart. He knows that your interest in the supernatural side of heaven is because you're designed that way. He gets you. He'll teach you how to love along the way. Never let your self-judgment stop you from praying for people in the hopes of giving them a healthier and fuller life, which in turn will draw them closer to the heart of the Father. That's part of it—don't let *you* get in the way of *him*. He said it, go do it, be happy.

WHEN

For example, the other day I was out driving for a rideshare company and five girls got in the car with a bottle of champagne. The girl beside me asked another girl to hold it because her arm was too sore, so I held out my hand and told her to take it because I had a healing touch. I then asked her what she was feeling in her arm—tingling, cold, heat—and she was amazed to feel tingling and asked me what was going on. All the other girls fell silent. I told her to check out her arm for her pain level and it had gone down from a 6 to a 4, so I took her hand again. After a few more seconds she tried it out again and her pain level was at a 0. Apparently she'd had surgery on it six months previously and it had been painful ever since.

I told her that it was simply the presence of God in me flowing through to heal her shoulder, and that if she ever needed more healing to just ask Jesus to do the same again.

It's awesome to have the honor of revealing him in those moments.

WHO

Don't be afraid. When fear holds you back, you're comparable to a bank account a friend has deposited millions of dollars into, and you're unwilling to make a withdrawal because you're afraid of your ways of spending. What a waste! So when I talk about flowing in the gifts of the Holy Spirit, it's not just for you, it's for humanity.

The first time the Holy Spirit came in bodily form, he came like a dove. Since the resurrection, he takes on bodily form in us.
~ Solape Osoba

You're the living epistle of God's heart of love. People don't have to wait for angels to stir up a pool anymore, they just need to wait for you to walk by.

TRUTH

What is the truth about praying for physical healing? Mull over the following Scriptures and write down anything God shows you through them.

"They will lay their hands on the sick, and they will recover" (Mark 16:18).

"Jesus said, 'Someone touched me, for I perceive that power has gone out from me'" (Luke 8:46).

PHYSICAL HEALING

"He cast out the spirits *with a word* and healed *all* who were sick ... '*He* took our illnesses and bore our diseases'" (Matthew 8:16-17, emphasis mine).

"'Lord, *if you will*, you can make me clean.' And Jesus stretched out his hand and touched him, saying, '*I will*; be clean.' And immediately his leprosy was cleansed" (Matthew 8:2-3, emphasis mine).

"The prayer of faith will save the one who is sick, and the Lord will raise him up ... Pray for one another, that you may be healed" (James 5:15-16).

FINISH THESE SENTENCES

I'd like to/rather not walk up to strangers and offer to pray for healing because

I think Jesus sees physical healing as

I think the Holy Spirit will/will not heal through me because

When I think about Jesus saying we'd all do greater things than he did, I

I'm going to practice praying for physical healing for people more by

My motive for seeing people healed is

PREPARATION

Ask God for his power and love to flow through you.

Pray every chance you get. Be open for opportunities.

Get in an environment that encourages practice and has people who can help you improve. Many churches have healing teams you can learn from and join.

APPROACHING PEOPLE

You might find you have more faith for one sickness than another, which makes it easier to step out and be brave when you see it.

Try to avoid using church language. Use words you know people will understand.

Write healing prayers for people in a private message or e-mail.

Offer to pray for people over the phone.

Ask friends at church if you can practice and lay hands on them for healing.

PRAYING

Keep it short.

Keep the time with them comfortable.

Ask people what they want prayer for.

Ask permission to touch the person's head or shoulders while you pray. It's okay if they say no, but healing is often transmitted by touch.

Keep your eyes open.

Don't pray while a person is working, for example, if you're at the mall.

Pray what God's Word teaches, not your doubts.

Tell the disease or the person's body what to do. Don't hedge. Be direct.

Ask people how they're doing and what they're feeling for clues of how to continue.

Don't quit early.

FLOWING WITH THE HOLY SPIRIT

Listen for what God wants to do. These clues can show up as intuitions, impressions, or feelings in your body. If you experience something, ask the person if he's experiencing that same thing.

Use all your senses. *See* the body part healed. *Know* where God is focused. *Listen* to what God is saying. *Feel* the pain level diminish or the healing begin to happen.

Be willing to work with God's creativity. Sometimes, for example, he'll have you put a hand on the arm or foot. At other times he might have the person put the phone on it, while at other times he might simply have you put your hand on the troubled spot and say absolutely nothing.

AFTER PRAYING

Ask if the pain level has changed since you started praying. Ask for a pain level percentage before and after prayer, or ask what number the pain is on a scale of one to ten.

If the pain has only lessened a small bit, ask if you can pray again (based on their comfort level).

Expect the person to ask how the healing came about. I usually say it was the presence of God flowing through me, and that God always wants to heal.

SAMPLE PRAYERS

Pain, leave this body now. You have no right to be here, and you must go back to the place you came from. Muscles and ligaments, I speak realignment and healing to you. Body, get back in line with the way you were designed to function.

or

Cancer, leave this body now. Go where Jesus sends you and never return. Holy Spirit, flood through _____'s body and bring healing to every single cell.

or

Digestive system, I speak peace and healing to all your parts. I speak regeneration and restoration to every cell.

NOTES

PHYSICAL
HEALING

Notes

PHYSICAL
HEALING

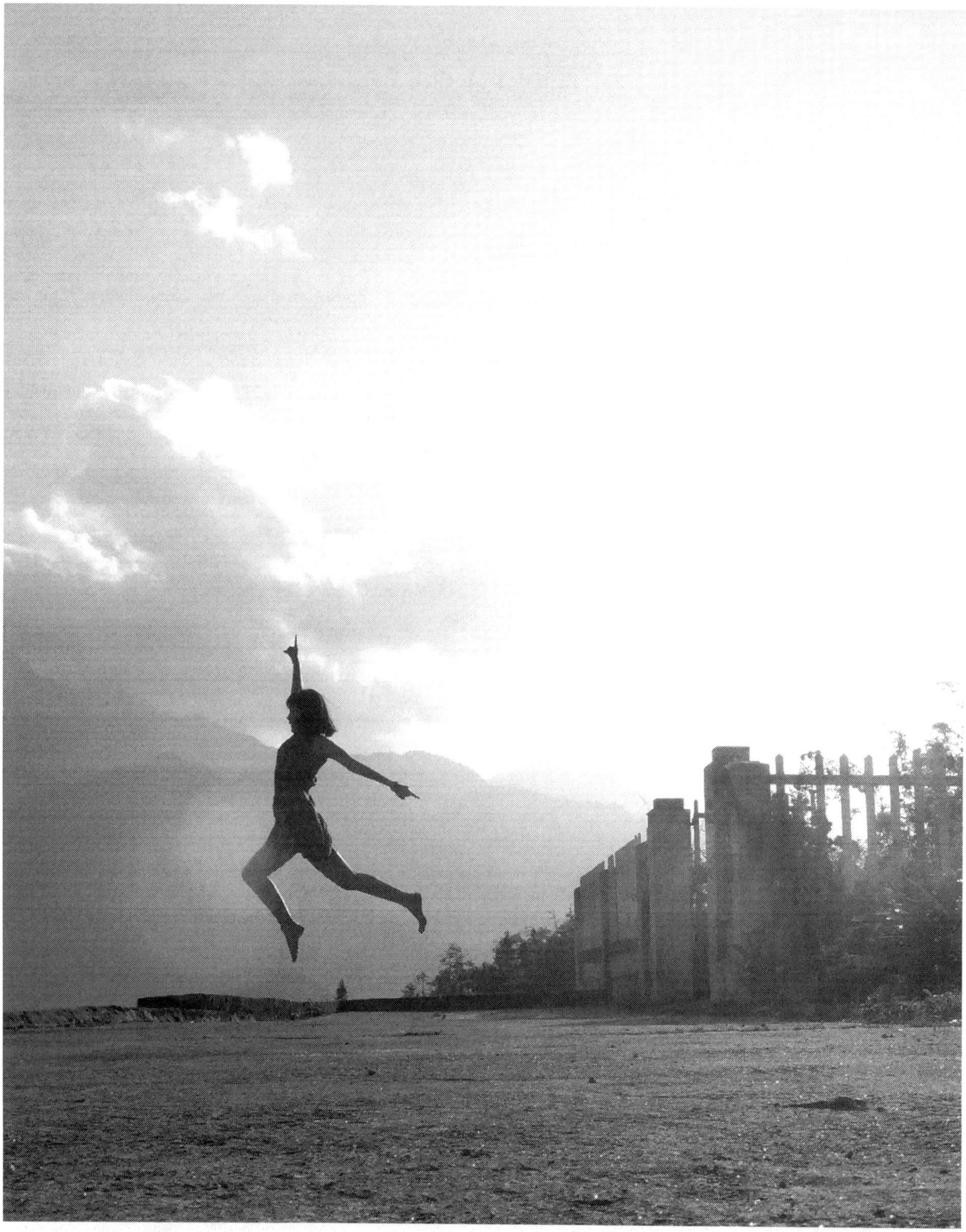

THE ARTS

My friend was suffering from cancer. She called me and told me she was praying with the words from Jeremiah 29:11 and asked if I could sing it for her. That Saturday in worship, the Lord told me not to leave without recording the song for her (she was not there, but was waiting for me to send her the song). He told me my singing would open up the atmosphere, so I turned to my two friends and told them what the Lord said. You could tell there was a "sweet something" in the air, and I was captured the whole night within it! After service, we didn't even go over the song; we just winged it and recorded it. (Talking about it still brings such a peace of God on me.)

My friend uploaded the song. She said she had not been able to sleep through the night recently, but she was so blessed by our song, she fell right to sleep. We got such a response from so many people after we put it up on YouTube— e-mails, stories, testimonies, messages—all about how it hit the spirit of fear they were swimming in and how God gave peace through that song.

~ Nadine

Before I headed to Mozambique, the Holy Spirit told me to pack paint, so I packed four full tubes of paint and a few bits of leftover paint. We got approval to paint in the prison in town, and within about twelve hours, three of us created an eight by nine foot optical illusion of a door in the prison wall. There are three stairs leading up to a golden path that goes straight back to a glorious sunrise. In the path, there is a small cross to represent Jesus as the invitation and the only way. There is actually a small hole in the wall that looks like a person on the path—beyond the cross. How perfect. As we brushed on the final details, a man stood up and said that on the outside it looked like a prison but on the inside, it was a church.

After we left, we received an e-mail saying that men were being healed and saved after looking at the painting! God opened the prison doors so that we could paint a door of hope and freedom in one of the most depressed, hopeless, dead-end places in that town—one that is still there but now ministering through the arts.

~ http://createsupernaturally.com/african-prison-mural

The spirit of the artist always shines through, and you can impact the hearts of those around you through your unique creative expression of God's love, whether it is through dance, art, words, or music. I have yet to meet someone who hasn't been touched in some way by a certain song, painting, dance, or performance.

SONG

Prophetic worship is a form of prophecy that is usually heard through spontaneous songs sung during times of corporate worship. A prophetic song is similar to a spoken prophetic impression from the Lord, only it can rhyme, and it's often sung as a message from God to us. Most prophetic songs communicate the Lord's heart for a particular individual, group, or situation. If you are the one giving the song, you have discerned what's on God's heart for those in front of you, and you help God's people engage in that.

"We were at a park frequented by drug users in Athens, Greece, and we met a guy who had really sad eyes. Someone on my outreach team put a guitar in my hands. 'Sing to him,' she said.

I sang songs of freedom and peace over him. He stared at me the whole time and cried, even though he couldn't understand what I was saying. The Lord was ministering to him. He told our translator that he didn't want to do drugs anymore. We all prayed for him to find a place to call home where he could be loved and not be on the street anymore."

~ Alyssa

Prophets often delivered their words with musical accompaniment in the Old Testament.

- "David and the chiefs of the service also set apart for the service the sons of Asaph, and of Heman, and of Jeduthun, who prophesied with lyres, with harps, and with cymbals" (1 Chronicles 25:1).
- "After that you shall come to Gibeath-elohim, where there is a garrison of the Philistines. And there, as soon as you come to the city, you will meet a group of prophets coming down from the high place with harp, tambourine, flute, and lyre before them, prophesying" (1 Samuel 10:5).
- "And Elisha said, 'As the Lord of hosts lives, before whom I stand, were it not that I have regard for Jehoshaphat the king of Judah, I would neither look at you nor see you. But now bring me a musician.' And when the musician played, the hand of the Lord came upon him. And

he said, 'Thus says the Lord, "I will make this dry streambed full of pools"'" (2 Kings 3:14–16).

> - Ephesians 5:18–19 connects being filled with the Spirit with singing. "Be filled with the Spirit, addressing one another in psalms and hymns and spiritual songs, singing and making melody to the Lord with your heart."

While I'm probably never going to introduce myself to the church visitor in song, prophecy in song can bring biblical truth in a strong atmosphere of the Holy Spirit's presence. As seen above, the Old Testament is full of references to its value. Five of the psalms command us to sing a new song to God, and each psalm is a song. Song of Solomon was written as a heartfelt set of songs prompted by Solomon's overwhelming love for a woman. Many scholars believe it can also be read as God's personal love letter to his bride. Even apart from the words set to the music, a rich presence of the Holy Spirit always accompanies a true period of prophetic song.

There's a distinct difference between giving a corporate song and giving a personal one. Most corporate songs encourage, comfort, and edify a group of people, whereas a personal song is more specific about things in a person's heart that need an application of love and hope. Prophetic songs act as a salve or a reminder of direction, and giving one is a powerful way to serve up the Father's love.

DANCE

Dance is usually seen in churches that encourage members to be led by the Holy Spirit in their various expressions of creativity. "Dance is the hidden language of the soul" (Martha Graham).[1]

"I think it's impossible to catch God's heart for someone else and not be profoundly impacted yourself. When I dance in worship, I consistently feel his joy, even if I am far from joy in that moment. You can't dance and stay in a bad mood for long."

~ Ashley

The Hebrew word used in the Old Testament for dance, *hul*, carried with it the idea of whirling and turning. Greek words used in the New Testament have to do with lifting up the feet or leaping with regularity of motion. In biblical times, dance was almost always an expression of joy and thanksgiving.

---

1. "Martha Graham Reflects on Her Art and a Life in Dance" (31 March 1985); republished in The New York Times Guide to the Arts of the 20th Century (2002), p. 2734

> *David danced and sang because he was happy about bringing the ark safely back into the city (see 2 Samuel 6 and Psalm 30). Miriam danced with other women after the waves killed off all the Egyptian army. She also sang a prophetic song that was to last throughout many generations as a reminder of the Lord's protection (see Exodus 15). Women danced when their men came home from war (see Psalm 149). When we dance in church, we flow in love, joy, thanksgiving, and praise. When we dance prophetically, we can express our love to God and reveal God's heart to people.*

Dancing is God's perfect way of helping us to express our matchless spirits. How happy can you make other people by being free? Google "Dancing Tommy" and you'll get a brief idea of what one man's journey into the freedom of dance can do for the world. Tommy used to be a drug addict, until an accident caused him to rethink his life choices. He started to dance on the streets around his hometown, and one day a group of vacationers filmed him dancing in the rain on Main Street. They posted it on YouTube and it went viral. Now Tommy is a dancing legend.

"Tommy is a dealer in smiles. He expresses the child that hides in all of us 'grownups'–the free spirit not yet caged by fear or social barriers. Above all, he is simply himself, and he brings this message: 'I'm free to be me and so is everyone else.'" [2]

CREATIVITY

The Holy Spirit and your spirit light up every piece of creativity you release. Some of you write and your words are inked into your readers' hearts. Some of you act or give spoken word performances or read poetry, and your body language and inflections act like a marinade, seeping into the souls of your audience. Some of you paint or draw or make striking jewelry, and your creations adorn walls and laptops and bodies with beauty that touches and heals emotions. You get to share your flavor of art with everyone around you—art that's as unique and memorable as you are.

ART

God's love of art and creativity is highlighted biblically—he placed a high emphasis on the need for skilled artisans to create the Tabernacle of Moses and to create the gold workmanship on the Ark of the Covenant (see Exodus

2. www.tommy-franklin.com

31 and Numbers 8).He wanted the art to display some of heaven's glory and beauty, and he still wants to do that today through us.

> *"I was healed of bipolar depression while standing in front of a hope painting. All my self-hatred, depression, and suicidal thoughts left. My joy continues to grow every day."*
>
> *"I was healed when I touched a picture with a word of knowledge for pain in the elbow, and when I prayed for someone else, she was healed too."*
>
> *"I felt my heart heal, and I also felt like I was stepping into my destiny—to minister to unreached and unloved kids."*
>
> *"My depression and anxiety left when I was given a picture of a cherry blossom."*
>
> ~ Testimonies after Bethel Supernatural Creativity Conference, 2011

Art has a unique way of bypassing the mind and going directly to the soul, and when artists combine their unique talents with the power of their relationship with the Holy Spirit, the results can be life-transforming. Prophetic art is simply an artist's capturing of something God has revealed that the artist then gets to share with others. Some pictures have pulled me toward them and kept me staring for a long time, and not purely because of the art itself. Just like the joy of seeing the hearts of people behind their behaviors, there is a profound sense of satisfaction in being spiritually fed by a painting or a drawing. People's self-protective guards can be so high that they miss out on everything you can offer. Viewing an art piece, however, requires no such protection. Let your art minister to their hearts without a word being shared.

> *People aren't afraid of a painting, but they might be afraid of you.*

WORDS

I love to write, and words have ministered to me over and over. The Bible has been a staple since I was small, and the words in it are truly living and active when they are mixed with the Holy Spirit's presence. I remember one time when I was feeling particularly lazy and I opened my Bible to read, "Awake, O sleeper, and arise from the dead, and Christ will shine on you" (Ephesians 5:14). Funny haha, God.

Some writers' prose can catch my imagination and cause my mind to swirl in many creative directions. It could be the way a setting is described, or the personality quirks of a character, or the breathtaking writing style, but whatever it is, the writer reaches into me and gives me life.

"The main way writing touches me is when I have the fresh perspective of another person that flips my comfortable definition of God and makes me stop. I freeze in that moment to take in another world of possibility and hope that I never imagined. I will often re-read those thoughts five or six times over a few days and let them simmer in my soul. I often step away from those moments with a changed heart and increased hope."

~ Brenda

Like Brenda, I can experience the same thing happening to me when I'm writing, especially if I'm in the middle of a short story. When I want to have the reader picture herself in the character's body and feel what she's feeling, I'll close my eyes and go there myself. That's the place I'll write from. I've had responses from many people saying how emotionally affected they were by a certain story I wrote, and I think the main reason is either that they feel understood, or they finally understand what's going on in a loved one. They gain empathy instead of only having their previous one-sided perspective on a matter.

The other thing about writing is that it can reach so many more people than conversation can. Every testimony about the goodness of God that is caught on video, in print, or digitally can be shared and re-shared, eventually touching people all over the world. Unreached nations finally have the opportunity to read fiction or nonfiction that sparks the knowledge of God's love for them. That's an immeasurable gift.

Think about the power of a note that lets a friend know you are praying for her, or an e-mail with a word of encouragement, or a book that opens someone's heart to friendship and community. Even memes have helped many people—photos or artwork with wisdom splayed across them. You may be such a social media aficionado that you groan when you see the same meme pop up on your browser yet again, but those familiar words could save a life.

FaithWriters.com is an online forum for Christian writers. They regularly receive e-mails from people who have been drawn to the site by members' articles. As one of the administrators quotes:

"**They** click on a link to our evangelism site and accept Jesus as their savior.

One man e-mailed: 'I literally was transformed and totally healed in an instant upon trusting in Jesus as my lord and savior. The love, joy, light, and peace I feel is way more than words or thoughts can express. This new life of being a true Christian who is saved, Spirit-filled, born-again, fully and truly converted by the living holy gospel of our Lord Jesus Christ, is going to carry my being further than anyone could ever imagine. It will be the most blessed, rewarding, and holy life in the Lord which I have embarked upon now.'"

His life will never be the same because one writer put pen to paper and shared something in writing.

FILM

Of everything that mimics real life and grabs your emotions, a movie is probably the most powerful. People respond quickly to a short clip or a movie scene because they can see, hear, and feel in the moment. A baby crying, a family dinner, a death, or a wedding—all can remind the audience of similar times now past. They might identify deeply with the sight of those events. The great thing about movies and other stage performances is that we can use them to bring hope and joy. We can represent a piece of heaven on earth. For example, do you recognize this line?

"**CARPE** diem. Seize the day, boys. Makes your lives extraordinary."
~ *Dead Poets Society*

We can write the scripts and find the actors who inject more life into a story with the light they carry, because it's not the words we speak but the Spirit behind them that reaches the heart.

We can leave the viewer resting in love.

Granted, there are far too many movies that should never have seen the light of day, but when you invest yourself as a writer or actor in a heaven-sent project, you invest in humanity. It's easy to criticize the efforts of Christian moviemakers. Let's shift that into encouragement and resourcing of the finances needed to bring excellence to that arena.

There's a difference between being talented and being a gift. Being a gift involves letting the Holy Spirit flow through all of your amazing talent and laying that double chocolate chip fudge sundae with ten toppings out on the table for all to benefit from and enjoy.

TRUTH

What is the truth about ministering through the arts? Mull over the following Scriptures and write down anything God shows you through them.

"He has filled them with skill to do every sort of work done by an engraver or by a designer or by an embroiderer ... or by a weaver—by any sort of workman or skilled designer" (Exodus 35:35).

"My heart overflows with a pleasing theme; I address my verses to the king; my tongue is like the pen of a ready scribe" (Psalm 45:1).

"The Lord ... will rejoice over you with gladness; he will quiet you by his love; he will exult over you with loud singing" (Zephaniah 3:17).

"And David danced before the Lord with all his might" (2 Samuel 6:14).

"See, I have called by name Bezalel ... and I have filled him with the Spirit of God, with ability and intelligence, with knowledge and all craftsmanship, to devise artistic designs, to work in gold, silver, and bronze, in cutting stones for setting, and in carving wood, to work in every craft" (Exodus 31:2-14).

FINISH THESE SENTENCES

I think singing to people or over them could

I value music as a way to show God's love because

When dancing, I

When I think about reading or writing inspired books or poetry, I

I'm afraid/not afraid to give people pieces of my artwork because

I steward my artistic gifts and share them with others by

DANCE

ON YOUR OWN:

Put on some great music and do the silliest dance you can think of. It helps to get all the awkwardness out of your system.

Dance to a song you love while listening, *seeing, knowing,* or feeling to see which parts of the heart of God you are expressing.

Get a scarf or other item that would add beauty to your dance moves and dance with the Holy Spirit as a way of expressing your own heart and worship to your Father.

IN A GROUP:

Team up and have your partner copy your silliest dance moves.

Do a silly moves dance conga around the room.

Invite dancers (anyone who loves to dance) up to the front to dance and then describe which parts of the heart of God they felt they were expressing.

Invite volunteers to the front. Have dancers dance around them as the dancers feel led and then have the dancers describe what they felt they were dancing.

SING

ON YOUR OWN:

Put on some instrumental music and picture yourself stepping into the Holy Spirit. Let your spirit come up with the harmonies and words to sing to him.

Picture yourself as a child and sing to your younger self as if you were standing at the throne of God delivering a song of love from the Father's heart.

Don't feel as if you need words to the tunes you hum or sing. You can sing healing tunes toward people, or sing happy songs to yourself and others.

IN A GROUP:

Put on the karaoke version of a well-known song and pass the mic around so everyone can make up lyrics to it.

Worship together for a bit and then switch to instrumental worship music to let everyone in the room sing alternative lyrics or harmonies.

Invite people to come up to the front to share their God-given corporate or personal songs.

I experienced an emotional healing on a day I was planning to commit suicide in 1987. I believe the Holy Spirit saved my life that day by bringing a song to mind which made me turn the car around and come back. I was admitted into the hospital and had prayer time alone (not a psych ward), and God healed me of the depression and suicidal feelings I'd been struggling with.
~ Laurie

DRAW

ON YOUR OWN:

No matter what your level of artistic talent is, draw whatever pops into your head. Color it, if you want to. Ask God what his message might be to you based on what you drew.

IN A GROUP:

Team up and draw a picture for your partner. Ask if it resonates with anything going on in the person's life, and then ask the Holy Spirit if there is any additional interpretation of it he would like you to give.

WRITE

Write a letter to the Holy Spirit expressing your appreciation of his presence in your life.

Read an excerpt of your favorite book and ask yourself how it speaks to your soul.

Post a story about God's goodness in your life, or one of your favorite testimonies, on a social media site.

Encourage a friend with a thoughtful text message or e-mail.

Notes

The Arts

Notes

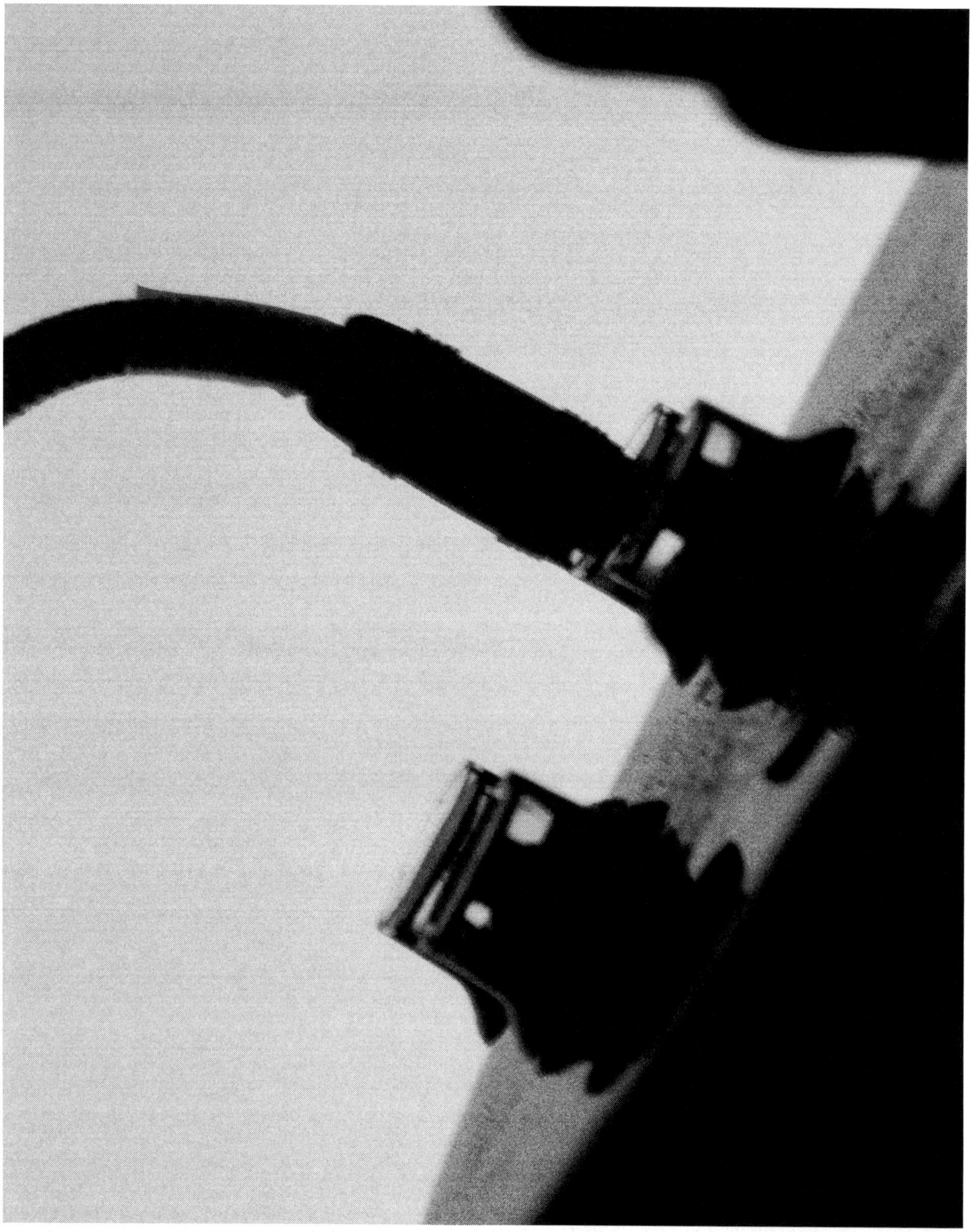

INTERCESSION

I was at a conference and the speaker asked us all to join in prayer with him and agree that an old friend of his would not die that day. His friend was in the ICU with multiple complications. Twenty-four hours later his wife contacted him to say that not only had the man's life been spared; he was also so healed that he had been moved out of the ICU and was eating dinner in a regular room.

~ Justine

I work in construction, and I was cutting bricks when I felt the Holy Spirit tell me to get on my knees and thank him for the angels who care for me and "lift me up in their hands, lest I dash a foot upon a stone." I wasn't even aware it was a verse in the Bible until after this incident happened. Later that day I was standing at the edge of some scaffolding when a big pile of bricks tipped off the plank of wood they were on and started to fall on me. They should have knocked me off my three-story-high perch, but as I watched, they parted in the middle to fall down around me. My coworker was dumbfounded, because he had watched the whole thing unfold.

~ Max

We had friends over for dinner one night, and at one moment my eyes fell on Misty and I heard in my spirit, "She has cancer." I said nothing, but the next day I began to intercede earnestly for Misty's healing from cancer.

Three days later, I heard from Misty that her doctor had found cancer in her colon, and the prognosis was not good. The doctor's course of action was to remove a very large section of her colon and hope for the best. I continued to pray intensely for Misty's healing until I felt the weight of this lift from me, two weeks later.

The next week, the doctor decided to do another scan to check the progression of the cancer before surgery. To his utter amazement, the cancer was gone, no cancer, nothing! I shared my story with Misty, who said, "Now we know what happened. We felt we were supposed to see what the doctors and God would do." I was so happy that I could play a part in God's plan for their lives.

~ Lyn

When most people talk or write about the gifts of the Holy Spirit, they highlight the gifts that are seen, the ones that demonstrate the power of God publically. I'd like to highlight the power of the unseen. Our thoughts, our words, and our actions all change the atmosphere around us. They can also disempower or empower heaven.

Prayer isn't all that attractive to believers these days. We're too busy and we don't believe in intercession when God is full of grace and he's got it all taken care of anyway. But that's not what the Bible says about prayer. Apparently it's a big deal, and it's very necessary in the day-to-day, heaven-touching-earth moments God wants to impact and flood with his goodness.

Prayer is usually thought of as the list of our requests and wishes for ourselves and other people. We sit or kneel and close our eyes and clasp our hands (so as to not be distracted), send up the list, and then we're done.

INTER-CESSION

Intercession, though, is when we act as a mediator between heaven and earth. We pray on behalf of someone else out of love and/or compassion. We intercede to "stand in the gap" for people, the gap being the distance or lack of relationship between the person we're praying for and God.

> "I saw God in heaven listening to the prayers of his people. Millions were praying and asking him to give them power, wealth, authority, and countless other blessings.
>
> I watched as he heard above all the prayers being prayed and earnestly gave his attention to the one asking to bring deliverance to his people, to be the vessel of deliverance to set the captives free. God's attention was captivated by her heart and reacted to her prayers." [1]
>
> ~ Victoria Boyson

The Bible says we're a holy priesthood (1 Peter 2:4), a royal priesthood (1 Peter 2:8), and a kingdom of priests (Revelation 1:5). In the Old Testament, the priest's responsibility was to stand before God to minister to him with sacrifices and offerings and to stand between a righteous God and sinful men and make the blood sacrifices. Now that we are all adopted into the family because the blood sacrifice has already been made, we are all holy priests resting in our intimate relationship with him. Because we are in Christ, there is no distance anymore.

1. http://boyson.org/articles/thepeopleneedadeliverer/thepeopleneedadeliverer.html

We are ready to pray for people to come into or be restored by relationship with him, and we have the honor of filling the lack of relationship with his love.

We get to pray God's heart into lives to bring life.

We are also royal priests, and royalty is descriptive of the kingly authority delegated to us as members of the "royal family," with legitimate access to the throne room of God (see Hebrews 4:14-16).

> *All the Old Testament priests changed history when they stood between God and sinful man and asked God to change his mind because they knew his heart. Paul encouraged the early churches to pray and intercede (see 1 Timothy 2:1). Jesus, too, interceded (see John 17:9) and still does (see Romans 8:34).*

Everyone can intercede, but there is a specific gift for some to devote their lives to intercession. Intercession is not expressly identified as a spiritual gift in the New Testament, so we are all to do it, but some people are gifted in such a way that their "prayer channel" seems to be static free. These people have a kind of prayer ministry where they spend a great deal of time in prayer in the full knowledge that God is listening and will answer them. They operate in faith and joy and are careful to focus and follow God's strategy.

FAITH:

We pray from a place of victory instead of into a place of victory. We are children of the King of Glory and the battle has been won. Victory is assured in these battles. If you're more afraid than you are hopeful, or if you expect defeat more than victory, you've made the devil bigger than God. The devil is just a fallen angel and we have the advantage—there are always 33 percent more angels than demons around (see Ezekiel 28).

Faith is just another word for trust, and we can trust God to fulfill his promises. Smith Wigglesworth said that he could get more out of God by believing him for one minute than by shouting at him all night. Everything we pray for is in his hands, and sometimes all we have to do is agree that he wants to give it to them and his goodness spills forth.

What if the whole point of prayer is that you don't pray to get an answer but you pray with the answer. ~ Graham Cooke

IDENTITY:

I've seen many Christians pray as if they are trying to manipulate God into doing what they want. "But God, didn't you see me help the assistant pastor with all those mailouts the other day? Didn't you see me give my yogurt to that homeless man? Didn't you see me get up at 4 a.m. for today's prayer meeting when you know I hate mornings?" Oh, he saw you all right! And he was probably questioning your motives, because you can't behave your way into his heart.

You're already there.

When we pray from a place of security in a Father who loves us dearly and who is always kind and good, we don't need to beg. We don't need to do anything to "make" him do what we want. Since when was prayer about getting him to do what we want anyway? Aren't we supposed to be praying according to **his will** ...?

> *Prayer and fasting is not a hunger strike. Fasting is declaring that you are more hungry for God than you are for food.*
> ~ Bill Johnson

JOY:

In the Father's presence is fullness of joy. From this place we begin to see from his perspective. As we see and understand his world, we are compelled to intercede from a place of love instead of despair.

> "Much of my exposure to prayer growing up in the church was lifeless, boring, and obligatory. It's not that anyone purposely made it like that. We just didn't know another way. And even in my adult years, many of the prayer rings/movements I've seen can tend to either focus too much on warfare and the devil or be borderline support groups for those in depression. A question I'd always asked myself is, "Where is the hope?""
>
> ~ William Matthews

God participates with us in prayer, which should blow us all away with happiness! God loves our minds and hearts and transforms our brokenness as a bonus when we pray with him (see John 16:22). David saw and knew and worshipped and received guidance during his intimate times of prayer and intercession (see Acts 2:25). Intercession lets us flush out darkness with intense doses of the goodness of God. We can be bold and consistent and starve evil of anything to feast on. Through our prayers we witness God's outpouring of love, healing, cleansing, and rebirth. I think God laughs a lot when we pray with our royal authority (see Psalm 2:4-6).

FOCUS:

We pray offensive prayers from his presence. When we speak our petitions and declarations into the atmosphere, authority and breakthrough come. From the intimate place with our Father, everything is birthed. We are not more aware of crises or problems than the awareness of God's presence. We pray from heaven down, from his perspective.

Dr. Andrew Newberg of Thomas Jefferson Hospital, Philadelphia, has been studying the effects of prayer on the brain for the last twenty years. He says his favorite observation, to date, has been his study of the meditative prayers of Franciscan nuns:

> "'The area of the brain associated with the sense of self began to shut down,' according to Newberg. 'You become connected to God. You become connected to the world,' he said. 'Your self sort of goes away.'"[2]

STRATEGY:

God will show you strategies to pray out of a place of victory. We have all the authority we need to tell the devil and his minions when and where to butt out and let the Holy Spirit get on with bringing heaven to earth.

> *Power is about catching a wave. Authority is about creating a wave. If God's not moving, I will move him.*
> ~ Smith Wigglesworth

Intercession is yet another facet of love, although it is the unseen gift—no one sees that the blessings of God fall on others because of your prayers. This is the one gift that goes unnoticed most of the time, but Jesus said to pray in secret. He knew our intimacy with him would bring us the greatest joy of all, and intercession is yet another powerful outflow of being in the secret place. Intercession is where things happen. We are the kingdom, bringing it to earth in our times of intercession. In him is the happiest place on earth.

---

2. http://www.nbcnews.com/news/religion/power-prayer-what-happens-your-brain-when-you-pray-n273956

TRUTH

What is the truth about intercession? Mull over the following Scriptures and write down anything God shows you through them.

"Let us then with confidence draw near to the throne of grace, that we may receive mercy and find grace to help in time of need" (Hebrews 4:16).

"In these days he went out to the mountain to pray, and all night he continued in prayer to God" (Luke 6:12).

"And he told them a parable to the effect that they ought always to pray and not lose heart" (Luke 18:1).

"Continue steadfastly in prayer, being watchful in it with thanksgiving" (Colossians 4:2).

I urge that supplications, prayers, intercessions, and thanksgivings be made for all people, for kings and all who are in high positions, that we may lead a peaceful and quiet life, godly and dignified in every way" (1 Timothy 2:1-2).

FINISH THESE SENTENCES

I think prayer is important/not important because

When I pray, I usually focus on

When I picture myself as a member of heaven's family with legitimate access to the throne of God, I

I think Jesus chose to pray a lot because

When I think about praying from a place of authority and power, I

I would like to change my prayers/prayer time by

TALK

Worship and thank God for everything good in your life. Starting a prayer time with thanks can set your spirit in the right frame of mind to receive and hear well.

Talk to God about what's going on in your heart and mind, as if you were sitting across from him in a coffee shop. [Some people say that it's sacrilegious to speak to God that way because he's to be feared, but he is also God the Son and God the Holy Spirit. We can speak to him as a friend.]

Be honest about the state of your heart. He's not fooled by any religious talk, and would much rather have you speak to him with no walls or mask in place.

LISTEN

Prayer should always be a two-way conversation. You're not a salesman, trying to talk God into doing something he isn't interested in. You're there to listen to his perspective and to ask him what his will is. He might want a different outcome than the one you are praying for.

Ask God if he would like to give you a prayer strategy for an issue you're bringing to him.

Ask God if there is any aspect of your prayer time he'd like you to focus on, e.g. a person, issue, event.

Be open to flow with the Spirit—he might have you dance or sing rather than talk at times.

ATTITUDE

Be sure to pray from a place of victory, with the attitude that you are a child of the king and as such, you get to tell darkness where to go and understand it has to obey.

Make sure you are interceding from a place of faith and joy instead of despair.

PRAY ACCORDING TO GOD'S GOODNESS

God's desire is always for healing and wholeness. When we pray according to those standards, we can remind God of his heart of love. Some of what Lyn prayed (see her testimony at the beginning of this chapter) was the following:

"The next day, I went before the Lord, 'What is your plan?' I asked. 'What do you want me to do?' I realized that if the Lord had pointed this out to me, he had something that he wanted me to do. I felt I was to intercede. I went before his throne of grace, thanking him for the way he had just recently joined Gordie and Misty together in marriage, for they had been married less than a year. I thanked him for the joy that Misty was bringing in Gordie's life, for Gordie had walked the painful path of his first wife dying from cancer. All of these things I had learned from them the previous night.

"I asked Father to spare Gordie this pain, pointing out to him that Gordie was just now beginning to learn how to laugh again. I continued to pray, thanking our heavenly Father for his perfect ways, ways that are beyond our comprehension, yet always the best for us. I also continued to point out to him the blessing Misty had been to Gordie and the joy that was evident in their lives. I continued to ask him to spare Gordie this added trial. I asked Father for Misty's healing. I then began to give praise and thanksgiving to my Lord, for I knew he had answered my prayers."

THANKSGIVING

Just as you started your prayer time with praise, finish with your focus on God's heart of love and desire to see heaven on earth. We have the honor of filling the angels' bowls with the incense of our prayers: "The twenty-four elders fell down before the Lamb, each holding a harp, and golden bowls full of incense, which are the prayers of the saints" (Revelation 5:8).

Notes

Intercession

Notes

REALITY

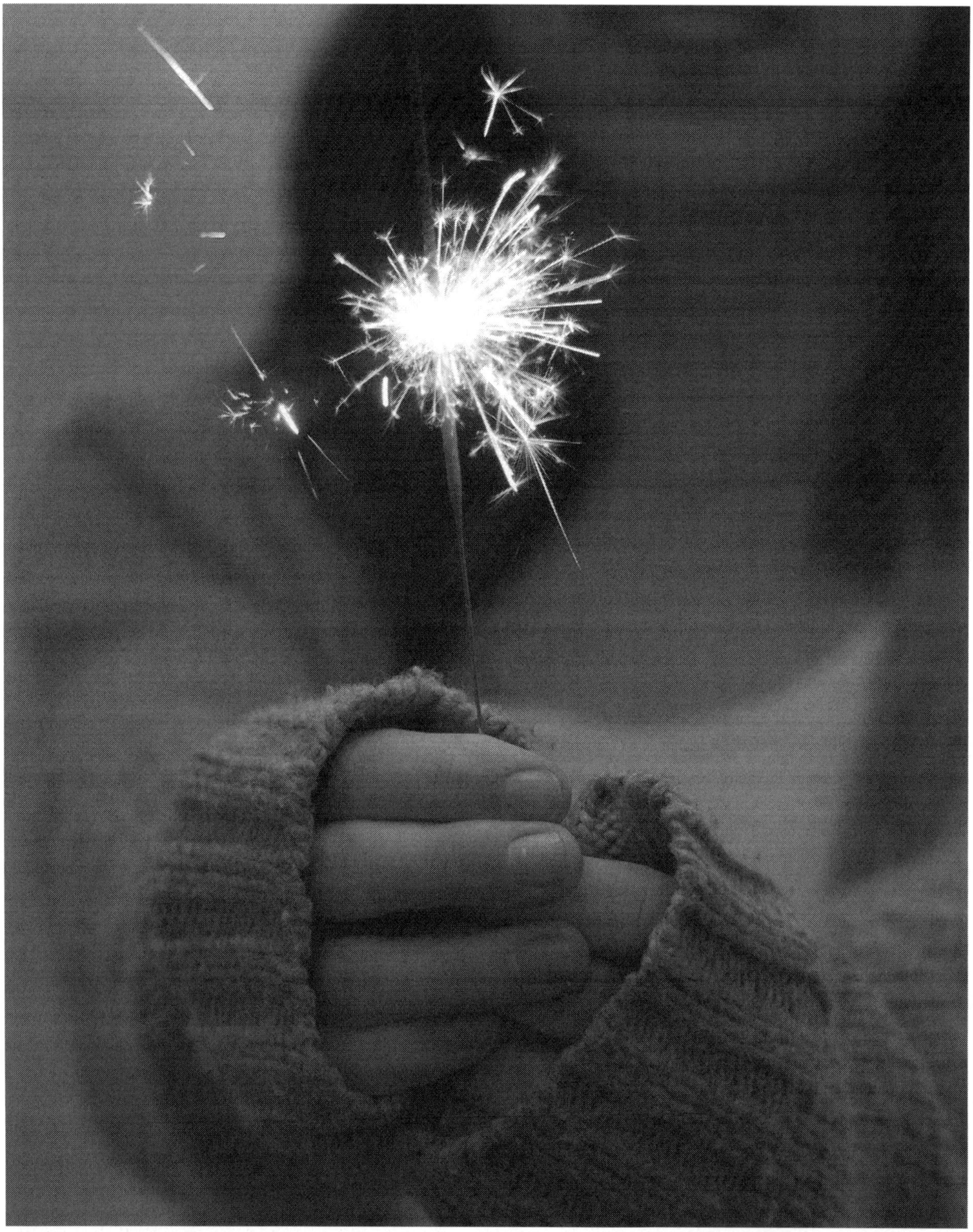

All the World

When I lived in Hawaii, I danced with a hula worship team. Using our hands and feet, we danced in unison, telling the story of God's goodness. During those moments, I felt as if the arms of God enveloped me. I was aware that my hands released a story, but also power to transform. Very often, as our group danced, people in the audience wept. People's hearts were touched and healed. Through the movement alone, there was power.

~ Traci

We were on a spiritual treasure hunt and had heard the clues "smoking and mall." As we were walking through the mall, there was an e-cigarette kiosk with a guy smoking at it. We told him we were on a treasure hunt and showed him our clues, and he was blown away.

We asked if he needed healing in his body. He was deaf in one ear, so we prayed and he was completely healed and removed his hearing aid! Then he turned around and asked us to pray for his back, and God completely healed his back! He then prayed with us to know this Jesus who just healed him. We were so blessed, we went back the next week to ask for his testimony, and his boss told us he had returned to construction because his back was healed!

~ Sally

I went with a team to love people at Burning Man this year. We stopped for the one everywhere we went, but imagine my surprise when I saw this on one of the Burning Man pages: "To the girl who held my hand in the temple and looked me in the eyes while I was crying and said, 'You got this,' thank you. I had just finished purging over a decade of self-hatred in the form of old journal entries and said goodbye, officially, to my abusive parents. You gave me a serious gift." It wasn't a long encounter, just quick, and I am stunned and amazed that something so simple could have made such an impact on her heart.

~ Terri

> "Kathryn Kuhlman strongly disapproves of anyone having the idea that this is a ministry devoted only, or even primarily, to the healing of sick bodies. This point she emphasizes in every service - for she believes sincerely that the salvation of the soul is the most important of all miracles."
>
> ~ Kathryn Kuhlman, *I Believe In Miracles*

I've had conversations with a lot of skeptics, people who are so afraid of other people's opinions that they shudder at the thought of running out into the streets to "convert the masses." I've seen the damage done by people with an agenda. Back in my teen years I was one of them, but my heart was good. My heart wanted everyone to know and experience the reality of God's love. He had revolutionized my life and I wanted him to do the same for others.

OUT IN PUBLIC

We used to do street skits and then have team members ready with a worksheet to see if the people who stopped to watch were going to end up in heaven or hell. Invariably, they would always seem to end up in hell (if you died tonight …). We used fear to sweep them into the kingdom. Did it work? On those days, yes. We got our saved numbers and our church numbers, but how good of a relationship can you claim to have with a community and God that use the fear of hell to have you start showing up every Sunday, Wednesday for meetings, Saturday for street ministry, Tuesday for one-one-one mentorship, and let's not forget the 6 a.m. prayer meetings? We were good at doing stuff, but we lived in a culture of passion laced with fear. We were standing up for Jesus, soldiers in God's army rushing the city and climbing the walls, with no focus on the love of God.

Some of you reading this have already joined teams doing street ministry. It's radically different, thank God. We no longer focus on hell, but on heaven. We are no longer fear mongers but love givers. Do we have an agenda? Yes—to let people know that God loves them, cares about every detail of their lives, and wants them to know him.

How is street ministry done these days? Where do you go? How do you minister love? It's good to start in a group and watch other people who have done it a few times already. You can get so creative when it comes to sharing love. Some ideas are:

Free prayer, free food, free hugs, dollar drops

Dream interpretation or spiritual readings—giving prophetic words

Spiritual treasure hunts—looking for people who match your prophetic clues

Singing over people or dancing

Giving out art with prophetic words on it

Spoken word performances

Looking for people in need of healing

EVERYDAY LIFE

I'm going to let you in on a major secret. All those videos, training sessions, group outreaches, and schools of supernatural ministry are created for one reason—to make the supernatural a normal part of life. The more "activated" you are in a safe setting, the more you practice, the more comfortable you become in creating heaven around you.

A homeless guy told me he had stomach and back issues, so I prayed and before the light turned green, all his pain and cramps had gone. Then I gave him $20, and he started to dance with joy because it meant he wouldn't have to stand out in the hot sun for the rest of the day.

~ Cindy

Because the Bethel School of Supernatural Ministry in Redding, California, has so many students, the city has become used to the offers of prayer. One woman even went so far as to call the office to complain that she went to the mall in the hopes of meeting with a healing prayer team and saw no one. Bethel's response was: "We don't always have teams sent out to the mall; we just have Bethel people who go shopping." The students and church members are so used to seeing God's goodness revealed that they are unwilling to let sickness walk by.

My hope is that that will be you, that everything in this book will become part of your tool belt—one you wear all the time and can pull from whenever you see something on earth that would not be in heaven. If we all pulled on heaven and displayed it on earth, Jesus's prayer of "on earth as it is in heaven" could become a reality.

THE GIFT

Everything about God and in God is a gift. Everything about us and in us is a gift to humanity. You very possibly don't think that's true, because even the way you chowed down on that bar of chocolate without sharing didn't exactly reflect the thoughtfulness and kindness of God (I'm still waiting). Nevertheless, if God sees you as a gift to others, than that means, wait for it:

You are a gift to others.

And stop arguing with the God-Spirit-Man! Either you believe him or you don't. The power gifts and the fruits of the Spirit are all already downloaded and installed, but many of them are waiting on you to activate them. And there you are, still struggling to share that piece of chocolate, aren't you?

First up, you're not a hopeless case. You're on an adventure of epic proportions and you have a full backpack with everything you need in it, but you haven't necessarily stopped to use a lot of the supplies. In that backpack is your best tool—one you'll need and use over and over—love.

Do you love yourself? Do you love your design, the unique way God made you? Do you love the way no one else can do that thing you do the way you do it? Here are three things you need to get straight in your head and never let go of:

> "You were born to be amazing. God was the painter, you are the painting, and Jesus was the model. You were saved when you believed in Jesus, but you got transformed when you realized he believed in you."
>
> ~ Kris Vallotton

Once you see the thoughtfulness put into your design and way of expression, you'll see it in everyone around you. Once you receive God's care and comfort and presence purely because he loves you, you'll give his care and comfort to others out of love instead of duty. Once you believe that God's greatest desire is for you to be loved, healthy, and whole because you are truly valuable just because you are, that will be your modus operandi for others. Love starts in you and grows outwards. People can plant seeds of love in your heart and mind, but they won't grow unless you receive them and give them room to grow.

"We accept the love we think we deserve"
~ Stephen Chbosky, *The Perks of Being a Wallflower.*

God is absolutely delighted with your being comfortable in your own skin with all your quirks and awesomeness—the way he's designed you to be—

and it's that perfectly designed *you* he wants to team up with and go on Holy Spirit adventures with. As Dr Seuss said, "But you … You ARE YOU! And, now isn't that pleasant!" Your distinct personality and passion match certain things in him in catalytic ways—ways that ensure God is on display while you have the time of your life in the process.

While this book is about how to fill up on the gifts of the Spirit so that you can become a veritable powerhouse of healing, prophecy, and the like, the point of being that powerhouse is to be a walking heart of God. Instead of making this about the list of gifts, how about making it the list of love? Everything you are, everything you do, everything you're here for starts and ends in love.

> *"Not all of us can do great things. But we can do small things with great love."* ~ Mother Teresa

EMPOWERED

And there you have it—all of the best parts of living in and loving God. We really do have the best life when we're one with him and always aware of his leading. We're surrounded by beauty, we have art and books, we have too many beautiful people around us to count. We get to be our beautiful selves and be happy about that. We get to love and be loved. We get to listen and see and know that he is God. We get to dance and write and sing. We get to interact with God and laugh with him and cry with him. We get to live out our days in the swirl of the Holy Spirit, in his fatherly arms, and in the friendship of Jesus. We are an empowered people. We are loaded with so much to give away, so much to serve with and make people's lives better.

Obviously I've only scratched the surface of what's possible when you walk with God. There are so many other gifts and miracles and wonderful things God does through us, but the main component in everything he does is us. He needs us to be ready and available and not scared. He needs us to know his voice so we can share it with others. He needs us to be just as aware of his thoughts as we are of our own. He needs us to recognize moments of opportunity to demonstrate his heart. He needs us to start today.

Remember that this is a journey, an onward path into his heart, and the more you know him, the more you can bring that depth of relationship to others. Remember that you're a team and that he's always running with you. The force is with you, young padawan (*Star Wars* reference). You have everything you need to fulfill your destiny.

TRUTH

What is the truth about being a light, moving in signs and wonders, and sharing the gospel with everyone? Mull over the following Scriptures and write down anything God shows you through them.

"He raises up the poor from the dust; he lifts the needy from the ash heap to make them sit with princes and inherit a seat of honor" (1 Samuel 2:8).

"And he said to them, "Go into all the world and proclaim the gospel to the whole creation" (Luke 6:12).

"I have come into the world as light, so that whoever believes in me may not remain in darkness" (John 12:46).

"As you sent me into the world, so I have sent them into the world" (John 17:18).

"Proclaim as you go, saying, 'The kingdom of heaven is at hand.' Heal the sick, raise the dead, cleanse lepers, cast out demons" (1 Timothy 2:1-2).

FINISH THESE SENTENCES

I want/don't want to share Jesus by means of prophecy, healing, or the arts because

I have/don't have an agenda for those I encounter during my day. It's to

I minister love by

My supernatural/spiritual tool belt has the following in it:

When I think about living an empowered life every day, I

I would like to grow more in the area(s) of

HOLY SPIRIT

Stay conscious of your presence in the Holy Spirit and of his presence in you throughout the day. I call it "living in the zone."

Whenever you think of him and suddenly want to speak in tongues, think of it as a healthy check-in and a mini praise session.

COMMUNITY

Hang out with other passionate Jesus lovers as often as possible. The more you allow others to love you, the freer you are to give love away.

Do stuff together—worship, pray for people, practise giving each other words, value the tool belt each person pulls from.

Encourage the sharing of testimonies every time you are together.

HEARING GOD

Listen to every positive thought that fills your mind.

Pay attention to the lyrics that pop into your head.

Watch for messages from God's heart to yours through nature.

Capture your thoughts and conversations with God on paper.

Practise seeing pictures in your mind for others and look for the messages in them.

Look at the clues in front of you to hear God speak.

DREAMS

Write down the details of your dreams, or record them. Talk to God about the ones you think he's talking to you through.

If you dream about a friend, ask God what to do with it.

Set up a public dream interpretation booth and offer to interpret the dreams of passersby.

PROPHECY

Share every word of encouragement, comfort, confirmation, direction, and inspiration with those you encounter, as the Lord leads.

Listen for clues before you go out on a "treasure hunt"—a group time in which you go places to look for the clues you wrote down, for example, "black T-shirt, snake tattoo, brother." Once you find the person that fits those clues, show him or her your clues and ask if there's anything you can pray for, or ask if you can give an encouraging word and name all the good things you see in him or her.

Pay for a booth at a local event and offer spiritual readings, tattoo readings, art readings, etc.

Practice, practice, practice.

HEALING

Always be on the lookout for sick and hurting people you can pray for.

Be brave.

When praying, avoid using churchy words. Make your prayer as natural as possible, and keep it very short.

THE ARTS

Dance, sing, paint, act, speak, create whenever possible. You'll shine the glory of heaven and touch hearts all around you when you do.

PRAY

Angels are empowered by our prayers, and we can shift atmospheres and circumstances with our words and agreements.

BE YOU

Have fun with the Holy Spirit and *be you! Be* you in him in you. Enjoy this most excellent adventure called the rest of your life and spread the love and joy of heaven as you go so everyone you touch can be filled with this fullness of life too.

Notes

Notes

About the Author

Sally Hanan is an Irish import to the US. She made the "perilous" eight-hour crossing back in the '90s with a husband and two young children in tow. Since then she has managed to homeschool her above average kids (who are obviously absolute geniuses and extremely good-looking) and acquire more "stuff" than she knows what to do with.

On a more professional note, Sally has been counseling people for over twenty years and is a certified life coach and a facilitator at the Texas School of Supernatural Ministry. She also runs a writing and editing business on the side, because she gets bored easily and she loves fixing words as well as people.

Other Books by Sally

Fix Yourself is a workbook designed to help heal your heart and mind in God's presence so that you can move into emotional and spiritual wholeness. Each exercise encourages you to reflect on God's truth and then apply it. The truth is that there is nothing wrong with your original design, and in Jesus you will find everything you need to be restored to your unique and magnificent self. This book will help take you there, or at least help begin the journey. Because this is in workbook form, it can be adapted for use in small groups, with a mentor, or in workshops.

I really like this and will use it with my pastoral and inner healing teams. This is an amazing workbook that will be great for groups, individuals, and married people; with prayers, reflections, and work assignments that chart out inner change and help you to see God in the light of his love for you.
~ Shawn Bolz, Senior Pastor of Expression58
Author of *The Throne Room Company* and *Keys to Heaven's Economy*

A blind girl has a gift; a father's heart breaks; a young boy in Africa might die; the step-children want her dead husband's money ... read these short snippets of fiction and be prepared to gasp, giggle, and groan. Sally Hanan's insight into the human heart brings a depth of richness to her stories, many of them written in a poetic style of prose that flows and gurgles like a country creek.

Her poignant crystal clarity of truth and honest point of view of meaning and simplicity gathers together in the smallest set of words for each short story .... These stories reminded me of just one word–HAIKU ....
~ Pierre Dominique Roustan,
author of *The Cain Letters*

Pastor Mike Schaefer is close to death from the life-threatening injuries of a skiing accident. His close, extended, and church families are determined to see him through. Joining forces to call on heaven and assail hell, they agree with one voice that he will not die but live to declare the works of the Lord. Read this emotional yet triumphant story of the faith of many and the day-to-day miracles of the God they serve.

I couldn't put it down! A great read.
~ Sandy Sheer, Co-pastor, Tulsa Church, Oklahoma

God's faithfulness to his Word and the power in it resounds throughout this book—one that is a true inspiration to us all.
~ Cindy Mansfield, Station Manager KNAT-TV/ SW Regional Manager, Trinity Broadcasting Network

Made in the USA
San Bernardino, CA
28 September 2015